The Story of Liverpool FC

LIVERPOOL FOOTBALL CLUB

Founded: 1892
Colours: Red Shirts, Red Shorts
Ground: Anfield Road, Liverpool 4
Telephone: 051-263-2361
Ground Capacity: 52,518
Record Attendance: 61,905 v Wolves, FA Cup 4th Rd, 2 February 1952
Record Receipts: £154,000 Wales v Scotland, World Cup qualifyer 12 October 1977
Pitch measurement: 110 yards by 75 yards
Honours: First Division Champions 1900-1, 1905-6, 1921-2, 1922-3, 1946-7, 1963-4, 1965-6, 1972-3, 1975-6, 1976-7, 1978-9, 1979-80; runners up 1898-9, 1909-10, 1968-9, 1973-4, 1974-5, 1977-8. Second Division Champions 1893-4, 1895-6, 1904-05, 1961-2. FA Cup Winners 1965, 1974; Runners up 1914, 1950, 1971, 1977. Football League Cup runners up 1978. European Cup winners 1976-7, 1977-8. European Cup-winners Cup runners up 1965-6. UEFA Cup winners 1972-3, 1975-6. Super Cup winners 1977
Record Win: 11-0 v Stromgodset, European Cup-winners Cup, 17 September 1974
Record Defeat: 1-9 v Birmingham City, Second Division, 11 December 1954
Most League Points gained: 68, First Division 1978-9
Most League Goals scored: 106, Second Division 1895-6
Highest League scorer in a season: Roger Hunt, 41, Second Division 1961-2
Most League appearances: Ian Callaghan, 640 from 1960 to 1978
Managers since World War II: George Kay, Don Welsh, Phil Taylor, Bill Shankly, Bob Paisley
How to reach Anfield: Buses 17D from Pier Head and 26 and 27 from Castle Street. Nearest stations, Bankhall and Kirkdale
Address of Supporters Club: 212 Lower Breck Road, Liverpool

The Story of LIVERPOOL FC

Anton Rippon

Moorland Publishing

Picture Sources. Illustrations have been provided by: Colorsport: p13 (RHS), 15 (LHS), 17-19, 21, 25-6, 33, 47-9, 53 (bottom), 63-5, 71, 73, 75, 77-8, 87, 90-1; Liverpool Daily Post & Echo Ltd: p12, 13 (LHS), 14, 15 (RHS), 16, 23-4, 27-32, 34-7, 42-6, 50-2, 53 (top), 54-62, 67-70, 80-1, 83-4, 86, 88, 92.

 British Library Cataloguing in Publication Data

Rippon, Anton
 The story of Liverpool FC.
 1. Liverpool Football Club - History
 I. Title
 796.33'463'0942753   GV943.6.L55

 ISBN 0-903485-98-2

ISBN 0 903485 98 2

© Anton Rippon 1980

All rights reserved. No part of this publication may be reproduced, stored in a retrieval system, or transmitted in any form or by any means, electronic, mechanical, photocopying, recording or otherwise, without the prior permission of Moorland Publishing Company Ltd.

Typeset by Alacrity Phototypesetters,
Banwell Castle, Weston-super-Mare, Avon
and printed in Great Britain by
Redwood Burn Ltd, Trowbridge & Esher
for Moorland Publishing Co Ltd,
PO Box 2, Ashbourne, Derbyshire DE6 IDZ

1892-1950

IN THE BEGINNING

Liverpool supporters will always find it hard to admit that their world famous club had its origins in their most deadly rivals, Everton; for on Merseyside you are born either for the Super Reds of Anfield or the Toffeemen of Goodison Park — and the allegiance to one or the other is carried to the grave. It is a fact, however, that although Liverpool have completely outshone their First Division neighbours over the past decade and more, there would have been no Liverpool Football Club at all had it not been for a split in the ranks of the older Everton club. And whereas many Football League clubs can look back to dim and romantic foundations among the gas lamps of Victorian England, Liverpool FC was founded with the immediate intention of rivalling Everton. Liverpool became a professional outfit and a limited company on its inception; the Reds were founded to succeed — and succeed they have. Incidentally, it may also come as something of a shock to devoted Liverpool supporters that their team started out by wearing the blue which Everton now sport — and it was Everton who wore 'ruby' shirts.

Liverpool FC owes its existence to a former Lord Mayor of Liverpool and a man who was at one time known as 'King John of Everton'. If 'King John' had succeeded in his original plans, then there would have been no Liverpool FC — and yet he was the man who eventually founded the club which was to become perhaps *the* most famous in the world of soccer. He was John Houlding, who besides being Lord Mayor of the city, was also an alderman, JP, brewer and the man who owned the site of Anfield stadium.

It was to Anfield that Everton moved in 1884 — having been formed as St Domingo's Sunday School in 1878 — and as their landlord, Houlding was a staunch supporter of the club. He was a leading light when Everton became one of the original twelve clubs which made up the Football League in 1888 and had it not been for a clash of personalities, Everton would probably still be playing at Anfield, a prospect which must horrify present-day Liverpool fans, and there may well have been no second club in the city.

But Houlding found himself in a dispute concerning the rent which Everton were paying him for the use of Anfield and very soon the rift between the majority of the Everton members and the 'King' of their club was so great that the rival faction bought some land and moved their club to its present home at Goodison Park. Houlding was not a man to be beaten that easily and he decided that 'Everton' would continue at Anfield with a new team and a new club. The football authorities had other ideas and in February 1892 the Football League ruled that 'Everton' was the club which played at Goodison Park. The name was the right of the majority of members. Even an appeal to the Football Association failed to alter the situation and Houlding found himself cut off from the club which he had cherished for so long. But he did not remain out of football for more than a few days. On 15 March 1892, he launched a new club called Liverpool Football Club. Even then, the right to use the name was challenged because there was already a Rugby Union side by the same name. Houlding simply added the word 'Association' to his club — and Liverpool AFC were in business, complete with a £500 permanent 'loan' from their founder.

That first season of 1892-3 was one of mixed fortunes for Liverpool. On the field nothing could go wrong and the side swept away with the Lancashire League Championship and the Liverpool District Cup. Off the field Liverpool had both trophies stolen and it cost them nearly £130 to replace them. In addition, attendances were poor and while Everton were finishing third in the First Division behind Sunderland, the champions, and Preston North End, football at Anfield was not paying its way, even allowing for the tremendous start which the Liverpool team had made.

The early history of almost all the clubs in the Football League is littered with examples of sporting philanthropists like John Houlding and even when he faded from the Liverpool scene at the end of that first season, there was already a man to assume his mantle. John McKenna was a self-made man. He had come to Liverpool from Ulster as a nine-year-old and had worked his way up from grocer's errand boy to successful businessman. Like

---

When John McKenna applied for the Football League by telegram, the club secretary W. E. Barclay was opposed to the move. He was unaware that a telegram had been sent in his name until he received the reply: 'Liverpool elected. Come to London at 3 pm tomorrow to arrange fixtures.'

Houlding, McKenna was a keen soccer devotee and his business skills were welcomed warmly onto Liverpool's management committee. With the demise of Houlding, McKenna decided that there was only one place for Liverpool FC and that was in the Football League. An application to the League for that inaugural season had been turned down, thus forcing Liverpool to begin their career in the Lancashire League. But McKenna was adamant that the club would gain admission to the Second Division for 1893-4.

John McKenna, the man who steered Liverpool into the Football League in 1893.

His first task was to strengthen the Liverpool team which had already pulled off a local 'double' and he went to Scotland and came back with the signatures of no less than *thirteen* players. New names abounded at Anfield. John McBride, Duncan McClean from Renton; Malcolm McVean from Third Lanark; the two McQueens — Matt and Hugh — joined McCartney, Wylie, McOwen, McQue and Kelso on the Liverpool payroll. Thus strengthened, Liverpool made a second application for the Football League, boosted by the knowledge that the Second Division was to be increased in size from twelve to fifteen clubs. Yet Liverpool were only accepted by the demise of another neighbouring club when Bootle resigned having spent just one season in the League when they finished eighth in the Second Division. The club's directors decided that there was not enough support for the club to continue — despite the fact that they were a reasonably well-known name in football at that time. With Accrington resigning from the First Division there was now room for Liverpool and they joined an unlikely-looking Second Division which then boasted such teams as Burton Swifts, Northwich Victoria, Rotherham Town, Middlesbrough Ironopolis (no relation to the present Middlesbrough side), Small Heath and Ardwick — both of whom would eventually become names to

rival that of Liverpool. Other newcomers to the Second Division of that far-off season were Woolwich Arsenal, the only representatives south of Birmingham.

> *Liverpool's first-ever captain was Andrew Hannah, a former Everton player, while John McKenna became President of the Football League in 1910 and was later a Vice President of the Football Association.*

Liverpool began their career in the Football League in truly sensational fashion. In all the matches they played — League and Cup — Liverpool lost only five times, winning twenty-two and drawing six of their twenty-eight Second Division matches to take the title eight points clear of second club Small Heath. Their campaign started with a 2-0 win at Middlesbrough and when League soccer was first played at Anfield, Lincoln City were beaten 4-0 before some 5,000 spectators. In the FA Cup, Liverpool reached the quarter-finals before losing 3-0 at Bolton Wanderers, having on the way disposed of Preston North End, First Division champions and FA Cup winners of 1888-9.

> *Liverpool's Second Division Championship-winning side of 1893-4 was: McOwen, Hannah, McClean, McCartney, McQue, McBride, Gordon, McVean, Bradshaw, McQueen (M), McQueen (H). Two years later, Liverpool won the Second Division title again with this line-up: Storer, Goldie, Battles, McCartney, McQue, Cleghorn, McVean, Ross, Allan, Becton, Bradshaw.*

The Second Division table for Liverpool's first-ever Football League season makes interesting reading in comparison with today's:

		P	W	D	L	F	A	Pts
1	Liverpool	28	22	6	0	77	18	50
2	Small Heath	28	21	0	7	103	44	42
3	Notts C	28	18	3	7	70	31	39
4	Newcastle	28	15	6	7	66	39	36
5	Grimsby	28	15	2	11	71	58	32
6	Burton S	28	14	3	11	79	61	31
7	Burslem PV	28	13	4	11	66	64	30
8	Lincoln	28	11	6	11	59	58	28
9	Woolwich A	28	12	4	12	52	55	28
10	Walsall TS	28	10	3	15	51	61	23
11	Mid Iron	28	8	4	16	37	72	20
12	Crewe	28	6	7	15	42	73	19
13	Ardwick	28	8	2	18	47	71	18
14	Rotherham T	28	6	3	19	44	91	15
15	North Vic	28	3	3	22	30	98	9

But having topped the Second Division at the first attempt, Liverpool were not automatically assured of promotion and they had to play a Test match against Newton Heath, the bottom club in the First Division. Newton Heath became Manchester United and in this first encounter between two clubs destined to become the most feared in English soccer, Liverpool triumphed to take their place in football's top flight — after only two full seasons in operation and alongside their old rivals Everton, the team from which they had been spawned.

The first-ever Merseyside 'derby' matches between the two sides set the scene for the epic struggles which were to follow in ensuing years. At Goodison Park, 44,000 fans saw Everton win 3-0; at Anfield, 27,000 packed in to witness a 2-2 draw. But towards the end of that season attendances dropped rapidly and Liverpool dropped with them. Bedevilled by injuries, Liverpool sunk to bottom place in the table and after losing the Test Match with the Second Division's top club, Bury, the Lancashire rivals changed places. For Liverpool, the glory had been all too brief.

> *When Liverpool lost their Test Match with Second Division Bury by 1-0, and so lost the fight to stay in the First Division, the Bury goalkeeper was sent off for 'kicking a Liverpool player in the abdomen'.*

Liverpool were relegated after one season in the First Division. The bottom of the table read:

	P	W	D	L	F	A	Pts
12 Small Heath	30	9	7	14	50	74	25
13 WBA	30	10	4	16	51	66	24
14 Stoke	30	9	6	15	50	67	24
15 Derby	30	7	9	14	45	68	23
16 Liverpool	30	7	8	15	51	70	22

John McKenna's remedy for this bitter reverse after only one season was to travel north once again and raid the football clubs of Scotland. Back he came with such players as George Allan who was signed from Leith and who became the first Liverpool player to be capped by Scotland before he died at the tragically young age of twenty-four; and a player from Clyde called Archie Goldie. From Preston North End, McKenna signed England international Frank Becton together with Jimmy Ross, a goalscorer with a powerful reputation in the Football League. Off the field, Liverpool's new president was the son of John Houlding and with a new stand seating some 3,000, Liverpool knew they had to do better.

Like their first season in the Second Division in 1893-4, Liverpool wasted no time when they found themselves back there in 1895-6. The standards between the two sections of the Football League must have been great because Liverpool were clearly not a Second Division side. They beat Rotherham Town 10-1 with George Allan scoring four, and Burton Swifts and bottom club Crewe were each beaten 7-0 on their own grounds. Ardwick became Manchester City and there was another team from the brewing town of Burton — Burton Wanderers. But the names — new and old — all came the same to Liverpool as they romped away with the title, finishing level on points with Manchester City but scoring 106 goals (forty-three more than City) to take the championship by a vastly superior goal average. Only Darwen managed to take a point from Anfield when they forced a goalless draw with the Liverpool club which was now striking fear into the hearts of opponents.

Top of the Second Division at the end of 1895-6 – Liverpool's third season in the Football League – looked like this:

	P	W	D	L	F	A	Pts
1 Liverpool	30	22	2	6	106	32	46
2 Man City	30	21	4	5	63	38	46
3 Grimsby	30	20	2	8	82	38	42
4 Burton W	30	19	4	7	69	40	42
5 Newcastle	30	16	2	12	73	50	34

Even after taking the title so convincingly, Liverpool still had to go through the Test Match routine with games against Small Heath and West Bromwich Albion but this they did with flying colours, and season 1896-7 saw Liverpool back in the First Division once more, this time sporting for the first time the red shirts which were to become so famous throughout the world and which replaced the club's original blue and white quarters.

Liverpool's runaway attack found things more difficult against the better class defences of the First Division, but this time there was to be no speedy return. Instead, while they certainly did not set the country alight, Liverpool maintained a healthy fifth position, winning twelve of their thirty games and scoring forty-six goals. They finished streets behind the champions, Aston Villa, who topped the table with forty-seven points, but another three points would have lifted Liverpool level with the First Division runners-up Sheffield United. It was a much improved performance.

In the FA Cup, however, Liverpool looked like doing really well. In the first round of the competition, Liverpool beat Burton Swifts 4-3 in an exciting game at Anfield; in the second round they won 2-1 away to West Brom, and in the third round—

the quarter-finals — a 1-1 draw at Nottingham Forest brought the Nottingham side to Liverpool where they went down by the only goal of the match and Liverpool were into the semi-finals for the first time in their history. In the semi-final Liverpool met Aston Villa at Bramall Lane, home of Sheffield United, while all Merseyside was agog at the thought of an all-Liverpool FA Cup Final at Crystal Palace because, in the other semi-final, Everton were playing Derby County at Stoke. Alas, it was not to happen. Although Everton beat Derby 3-2, Liverpool could not pull off the second part of what would have been a unique city 'double'. Over 30,000 spectators saw Villa win 3-0, ready to go on to do the 'double' of First Division Championship and FA Cup. Liverpool had been outplayed on the day and yet it was a major step forward for a team formed only five years previously.

Liverpool made steps in other directions as well. The international selectors began to look at their team and Harry Bradshaw played outside-left for England in their 6-0 win over Ireland at Nottingham on 20 February 1897; Frank Becton played in the next match against Wales at Sheffield on 29 March; and George Allan was capped in Scotland's 2-1 win over England at the Crystal Palace on 3 April. They were to be the first of an illustrious line of Liverpool players who have answered their country's call, although Allan returned to his native Scotland and a short spell with Celtic, before he came back to Anfield in 1898 where he died from a lung complaint.

Season 1897-8 followed a similar pattern to the previous campaign, so far as Liverpool were concerned. They finished lower in the First Division — ninth — but still with a reasonably respectable record, and in the FA Cup, they reached the last eight. In the first round Liverpool entertained the unlikely sounding Hucknall St John's and beat the Nottinghamshire side 2-0 (the first round of 1897-8 also sported such teams as Long Eaton Rangers, New Brighton Tower and Gainsborough Trinity). In the next round Liverpool were held to a goalless draw by Second Division Newton Heath — the embryonic Manchester United — before winning the replay 2-1 in Manchester. This brought Liverpool a home tie with Derby County in the quarter-finals, but the Reds could not finish the job at Anfield and Derby were happy to go back to the Midlands with a 1-1 draw. The following week, Steve Bloomer helped Derby to a handsome 5-1 win and Liverpool's Cup hopes were over for another season.

But the following season was to stage an FA Cup semi-final of Titanic proportions — and Liverpool were totally involved. Indeed, it was to be Liverpool's best campaign in League and Cup since they took up arms. They finished second in the First Division and ran the champions Aston Villa close,

right to the final matches, before Villa inched away to take the title with just two points to spare, following an epic last game which the fixture planners could not have foreseen would have such importance. On the very last day of the season, both Liverpool and Villa were level with forty-three points apiece — and their final match was against each other at Villa Park! A record Football League attendance of 41,357 paid around £1,500 to see the championship decided. Alas, the game's billing far outreached its eventual spectacle. Villa score five times inside half-an-hour and the 5-0 scoreline gave them the First Division title with time to spare.

In the FA Cup, Liverpool beat Blackburn Rovers — still a famous name — in the first round, winning 2-0 at Anfield, and then beat Newcastle United 3-1, also at home. In the quarter-finals the Reds went to West Brom and beat the Throstles 2-0, a result which gave them a semi-final tie with Sheffield United at Nottingham. The scoreline stuck at 2-2 and the sides moved to Bolton where Liverpool twice surrendered a two goal lead before allowing Sheffield to come back to 4-4. The following Monday afternoon Liverpool and Sheffield tried yet again, this time at Manchester's Fallowfield where many of the 30,000 crowd spilled onto the field and the referee had to abandon the game without any score. The show and the players moved down the road to Derby and eventually there was a result. After three and a half matches (counting the abandoned tie) Sheffield scored the only goal of the game at the Baseball Ground to dump Liverpool out of the semi-final. The struggles with Sheffield United were not confined to the FA Cup in 1898-99. In a First Division match between the two clubs there was a bizarre incident when United's twenty-stone goalkeeper Billy Foulkes upended Liverpool's George Allan and stood him on his head, much to the annoyance of the Anfield crowd!

> *Liverpool signed 'Rab' Howell from Sheffield United. Born in a caravan, Howell is probably the only true-blooded Romany ever to play for England. He played one match while with United and when on Liverpool's books, appeared at centre-half against Scotland in Birmingham on 8 April 1899. He returned to his caravan when his playing days were over.*

Despite the disappointments of the FA Cup defeat and the final humiliation at Villa Park which cost Liverpool what would have been the first of many First Division championships, the Reds under John McKenna could be satisfied. They had overtaken Everton, who finished fourth in the table and who were knocked out of the FA Cup in the second round, and that in itself was sweet revenge after the trials and tribulations from which Liverpool was born out of the Goodison club's rebel faction.

If Liverpool's nineteenth-century supporters had been disappointed, perhaps frustrated, with their side's performance in 1898-9, their hopes and dreams were more than fulfilled two seasons later when in 1900-01, Liverpool took the First Division Championship at last. This time it was the Reds turn to finish two points clear, with Sunderland filling the runners-up spot. The second stage of Liverpool's reformation had begun in August 1896 when McKenna signed up Tom Watson, the secretary of Sunderland. Watson became secretary-manager of Liverpool and it was he who was responsible for the signing of Alex Raisbeck, a centre-half who went on to become one of the best players ever to have pulled on the blue shirt of Scotland.

> *A 19th-century book called* Association Football and The Men Who Made It *described Liverpool's Alex Raisbeck as 'like an intelligent automaton, fully wound up and ready to last through the longest game on record... Swift, rapid movement, fierce electrical rushes are to him an everlasting delight.'*

Raisbeck missed only three matches as Liverpool went on to take the First Division Championship, dropping only three points out of the last twenty-four to finish with forty-five. Liverpool's average attendance edged the 18,000 mark and although Notts County knocked them out of the FA Cup in the first round, Liverpool could look back on that season and marvel at the way they had won the Football League Championship only eight years after their admission. Again, the title rested on the last game but this time, Liverpool did not face title challengers, but the already relegated West Brom, who they beat 1-0 to pip Sunderland at the post.

> *Liverpool won the 1900-1 First Division title like this:*
>
> | | P | W | D | L | F | A | Pts |
> |---|---|---|---|---|---|---|---|
> | 1 Liverpool | 34 | 19 | 7 | 8 | 59 | 35 | 45 |
> | 2 Sunderland | 34 | 15 | 13 | 6 | 57 | 26 | 43 |
> | 3 Notts County | 34 | 18 | 4 | 12 | 54 | 46 | 40 |
> | 4 Nottm Forest | 34 | 16 | 7 | 11 | 53 | 36 | 39 |
> | 5 Bury | 34 | 16 | 7 | 11 | 53 | 37 | 39 |

The dawn of a new century was as exciting for Liverpool as for anyone and yet a decision to make the maximum wage £4 per week with just a £10 signing-on fee (the signing-on fee lasted at that figure until well after World War II), affected Liverpool badly, as the wages at Anfield were far above that figure. Some estimates put it as high as £12 per week — which was staggering money in Victorian England. The League's attempt to introduce a limit was understandable. It was designed to make all the clubs equal and give everyone a fair chance to recruit star players. In effect, it meant that many footballers left the game, disillusioned at the prospect of a drop in wages. Liverpool felt the wind of change and in the season following their championship win, the Reds fell to eleventh place in the First Division, while Sunderland took the title and, horror of horrors, Everton finished runners-up, although there was some consolation in the fact that Liverpool knocked Everton out of the FA Cup first round, winning 2-0 at Goodison Park after a 2-2 draw at Anfield. In the First Division Liverpool also had the chance to run up a cricket score when Stoke City lost four players with food poisoning. The Reds won 7-0 and five of their goals were scored by Andy McGuigan.

> *The side which took Liverpool to their first ever Football League Championship in 1900-1 was: Perkins, Dunlop, Robertson (T), Goldie, Raisbeck, Wilson, Cox, Satterthwaite, Raybould, Walker, Robertson (J).*

The downward path continued. Liverpool were relegated at the end of the 1903-4 season — next-to-bottom of the table with only West Brom below them and having conceded sixty-two goals in thirty-four games. It was the hallmark of a declining team as Liverpool's goals 'for' tally dropped to forty-nine, and it was obvious that the team would have to be strengthened before it could hope to regain a First Division place for Liverpool. The fact that it was strengthened to such an extent that Liverpool not only came right back as Second Division champions, but went on to become the first club ever to win the Second and First Division titles in successive seasons, speaks volumes for the far-sightedness which has always seemed to run through Anfield.

An amateur forward called Jack Parkinson was recruited from his native Bootle and made an immediate impact with twenty-four goals in his first season; Sunderland's Richard Robinson came to Anfield and also scored twenty-four goals; and a further nineteen were put away by Sam Raybould who came from Chesterfield. Liverpool, in fact, scored in every game but one — a defeat at Bolton — and they scored seventeen goals in their last five matches. If Liverpool had improved the cutting power of their attack, they had also bolstered the defence with the signing of Sunderland's veteran goalkeeper Ted Doig, a man who had begun his Scottish international career as far back as 1887, although he was never an automatic choice for his country. Doig let in only twenty-five goals as Liverpool took the Second Division title two points clear of Bolton in 1904-5. Everton had revenge in the FA Cup, knocking Liverpool out of the first round after two games, with the eventual winning goal coming from Harold Hardman, later chairman of Manchester United.

> *When Liverpool took the Second Division and First Division titles in successive seasons – 1904-6 – the following line-ups served the Reds:*
>
> 1904-5: Doig, Dunlop, West, Wilson, Raisbeck, Parry, Goddard, Cox, Parkinson, Morris, Raybould, Robinson.
>
> 1905-6: Hardy, Dunlop, West, Parry, Raisbeck, Bradley, Goddard, Robinson, Raybould, Carlin, Hewitt.

The following season, with Everton winning the FA Cup by beating Newcastle United 1-0 in the final, Liverpool made it a great time to be a Merseyside football fan, with the First Division Championship going to Anfield when the Reds finished ahead of Preston North End, despite losing ten of their thirty-eight matches. The Reds finished four points clear of 'Proud Preston' — not a particularly big margin but still the biggest for several seasons in an era when the First Division title was never really settled until the last day. As well as that great goalkeeper Sam Hardy, another face made his impact that championship season of 1905-6. Joe Hewett began a sixty-year association with Anfield by scoring over twenty goals as Liverpool stormed the First Division.

Don McKinlay signed at Christmas 1909 and gave Liverpool almost two decades of loyal service.

Sam Hardy, one of the great line of Chesterfield goalkeepers. Hardy signed for Liverpool in 1905 and became England's first-choice 'keeper'. He was transferred to Aston Villa in 1912 and went on winning international caps.

Liverpool's second title was won like this in 1905-6:

	P	W	D	L	F	A	Pts
1 Liverpool	38	23	5	10	79	46	51
2 Preston	38	17	13	8	54	39	47
3 Wednesday	38	18	8	12	63	52	44
4 Newcastle	38	18	7	13	74	48	43
5 Man City	38	19	5	14	73	54	43

Apart from their first FA Cup Final appearance in 1914, and the First Division runners-up spot in 1909-10, the years leading up to World War I were not good ones for Liverpool Football Club, especially after their triumphs of the early 1900s. There were momentary flashes of brilliance, like the 7-4 hammering of the eventual champions, Manchester United, in 1907-8. But the side was on the wane and several players, including the redoubtable Raisbeck, were all nearing the time of their careers when they were thinking seriously about hanging up their boots. The Welsh internationals Maurice Parry, George Lathom and Ernest Peake were also past their best and only the lad from Bootle, Jack Parkinson, and goalkeeper Sam Hardy, had much to show for that lean period. Both Parkinson and Hardy were capped by England, Hardy — who had made his international debut against Scotland in 1907 — holding down his place in the England side from the game against Wales at Nottingham on 15 March 1909 to the match against Scotland at Hampden on 2 April 1910, a run of nine matches. Parkinson played against Scotland and Wales in 1910.

> *Liverpool's famous Spion Kop which was built during the first years of the twentieth century was named after a famous Boer War battlefield. The 'Kop' has become world-famous and is synonymous with Liverpool Football Club.*

Elisha Scott, another great Liverpool goalkeeper. Scott played for Liverpool for 22 years from 1912 to 1934, for most of that time rated as one of the best goalkeepers in the world.

The seasons leading up to conflict also produced some bizarre results for Liverpool, like their match against Newcastle at Anfield in 1909-10 when Newcastle were winning 5-2 at half-time before Liverpool staged the fight-back of the decade to win 6-5; or the Christmas Day of 1909 when Liverpool found themselves without a fit goalkeeper and wing-half Jim Bradley bravely took over Hardy's jersey and helped Liverpool to beat Bolton Wanderers 3-0. Liverpool beat Nottingham Forest 7-3 and, when they were invited to play the first match at Old Trafford, the Reds spoiled the Manchester United party by winning 4-3.

> *Liverpool became First Division runners-up in 1909-10. The top of the table was:*
>
> | | | P | W | D | L | F | A | Pts |
> |---|---|---|---|---|---|---|---|---|
> | 1 | Aston Villa | 38 | 23 | 7 | 8 | 84 | 42 | 53 |
> | 2 | Liverpool | 38 | 21 | 6 | 11 | 78 | 57 | 48 |
> | 3 | Blackburn | 38 | 18 | 9 | 11 | 73 | 55 | 45 |
> | 4 | Newcastle | 38 | 19 | 7 | 12 | 70 | 56 | 45 |
> | 5 | Man Utd | 38 | 19 | 7 | 12 | 69 | 61 | 45 |

There was another influx of new faces to Anfield over those years, including the arrival of a full-back pair that would give Liverpool almost two decades of service. From Scotland came left-back Don McKinlay, later to win caps for his country, and from London — although he had started his career much nearer to Liverpool, at Bolton — the Reds signed Eph Longworth. Longworth, too, became an international and was the first Liverpool player ever to captain the full England side. The Reds defence was further strengthened by the arrival of Gainsborough Trinity's Harry Lowe, and Bobby Pursell from Queen's Park, and a goalkeeper called Bobby Campbell from Cambuslang who replaced Sam Hardy, transferred to Aston Villa along with centre-half Bobby Harrop.

Liverpool also signed on two players from Everton, one of whom became a famous Red. Bill Lacey was an Irishman and the sort of player who could turn out almost anywhere. He came to Anfield in an exchange deal with another Everton player, winger Tommy Gracey, while Liverpool's left-winger Harold Uren went in the opposite direction. As far as Liverpool were concerned it was a smart piece of business. Uren failed to make an impression at Everton but Lacey played for Liverpool for sixteen years and won twelve Irish caps with them to add to those he had already gained at Everton. In fact, Lacey was still in the Irish team after he left Liverpool for New Brighton.

In 1911-12, two seasons after finishing runners-up in the First Division, Liverpool narrowly missed relegation, the issue only being settled when they beat Oldham Athletic in the very last match of the season. The following year, however, Liverpool managed to climb to twelfth place, although in two meetings with the champions, Sunderland, Liverpool conceded twelve goals and scored only twice, a statistic which went a long way to explain Liverpool's 'goals against' tally of seventy-one — the fourth-worst in the First Division.

Liverpool's last chance of glory before World War I came in 1913-14 when the Reds reached the FA Cup Final for the first time in their history. The first round started off with shocks for both Merseyside clubs when Liverpool were held to a 1-1 draw at home to Second Division Barnsley, while Everton were beaten by Glossop North End, a team even further down Division Two, losing 2-1 in Derbyshire. Liverpool won their replay 1-0 and in the second round they beat Southern League Gillingham 2-0 at Anfield. The Reds faced further Southern League challenge in the third round when they drew 1-1 at West Ham before bringing the Londoners back to Anfield and crushing them 5-1. In the quarter-finals Liverpool were at home to Queen's Park Rangers — of the Southern League again — and again the London challenge went, this time beaten 2-1 to put the Reds into the semi-finals.

They met Aston Villa at White Hart Lane, home of Tottenham Hotspur, and before 27,000 spectators Liverpool won 2-0. Their former goalkeeper

> *Liverpool's team for the 1914 FA Cup Final against Burnley was: Campbell; Longworth, Pursell; Fairfoul, Ferguson, McKinlay; Sheldon, Metcalf, Miller, Lacey and Nicholl.*

Sam Hardy was beaten by Jimmy Nicholl and Bill Lacey, and on Boat Race Day 1914, Liverpool had won through to the Final by scoring a shock win over one of the First Division's top clubs (Villa were to finish second that season). The Final was to be played at Crystal Palace against fellow-Lancashire opposition, Burnley, who had beaten Sheffield United after a drawn first game. To add to the occasion further, the match was to be attended by no less a personage than King George V, although the overall attendance had dropped to 72,000 as neither Liverpool nor Burnley were considered fashionable teams.

Those who stayed away perhaps knew something for the Crystal Palace pitch was bone-hard and each time the ball bounced, it sent up little clouds of dust. It was a surface far from conducive to good football and the game never lived up to the Cup Final billing. McKinlay replaced the injured Lowe in the number six shirt of Liverpool, although Burnley's regular goalkeeper Dawson also missed the match and was replaced by a young reserve called Sewell. The game was settled by a lone goal, worthy of a far more illustrious game. Burnley's Bert Freeman snapped up a loose ball just after half time and smashed a fierce volley past the helpless Campbell. Although Liverpool had a couple of chances — both well saved by Burnley's stand-in goalkeeper — the match was over once the East Lancashire side had scored, and Liverpool's only consolation was a Cup-run profit of some £14,000. The Reds finished sixteenth in the First Division and another season drew to a close.

There was to be one more season before the war halted football. Although hostilities broke out in August 1914, the Football League decided to continue and Liverpool were knocked out of the FA Cup in the second round. They beat Stockport County 3-0 in the first round but Sheffield United then barred their path and won 1-0 at Bramall Lane. With a final First Division position of fourteenth, that appears to be a season which slips quietly into the history books and yet it is remembered for a match between Liverpool and Manchester United — both struggling to avoid relegation at the time — which rumours held had been 'fixed' so that someone could make a lot of money out of bets placed on the result.

The match was at Old Trafford on Good Friday 1915 and United, who were in deeper trouble than Liverpool, needed both points. For Liverpool, an improvement in their goal average was more important. Liverpool, however, wasted several chances, even to the extent of missing a penalty, and United won 2-0. The authorities could not help but overhear the rumours and an inquiry found that eight players were involved in the 'fix'. Liverpool's 'Gang of Four' were Pursell, Miller, Sheldon and Fairfoul

The Liverpool side which reached the FA Cup Final in 1914. Bill Lacey (second from right, front row) was part of an exchange deal with Everton. He went on to win 24 Irish international caps and played for Liverpool for 16 years.

— all of whom had played in the FA Cup Final twelve months earlier. They were suspended *sine die* along with a former Liverpool player who rejoiced in the name of 'Knocker' West. Sheldon and Miller had their livelihoods restored in 1919 but West had to wait until 1945, by which time he was sixty-two, before the FA lifted their ban on him.

With the war now entering its second year, the Football League decided to suspend the entire competition for the duration and Liverpool fans could only sit — probably in the trenches of Flanders — and dwell on the past glories of their Anfield heroes. Jack Parkinson, who scored thirty goals in 1909-10 to help Liverpool to reach runners-up spot in the First Division was one name which would continually crop up in their reminiscences, although an injury meant that Parkinson missed many matches which could otherwise have provided him and Liverpool with many more goals. The club had been formed by John Houlding to succeed and to a great extent it had done just that, with First Division Championships and an FA Cup Final appearance already to its credit. Certainly, the club went into World War I with the knowledge that when peace finally came, they had to march on into the new world carrying the hopes of thousands of Liverpool men.

BETWEEN TWO WARS

The first four seasons following the end of World War I were good times for Liverpool. They finished fourth in 1919-20 and 1920-1, and won the First Division title in successive seasons, 1921-2 and 1922-3. In the first peacetime season Liverpool, like all other clubs after four seasons of enforced idleness, enjoyed the benefit of some new faces on the playing staff. They included Tommy Bromilow, a wing-half who was to win five full caps for England before becoming manager of Burnley and Leicester City; Harry Chambers who also played for England — eight times in all — and possessed a shot as fierce as any goalscorer in the Football League; and inside-forward Tom Miller who won one Scottish cap before he moved on to Manchester United.

In 1919-20 Liverpool were a good way behind the champions West Brom, who finished with sixty points to the Reds forty-eight, but another couple of wins would have taken Liverpool into runners-

> When Scotland played Ireland in Glasgow on 13 March 1920, both goalkeepers, Bobby Campbell (Scotland) and Elisha Scott (Ireland) were Liverpool players.

Elisha Scott looking more like an ice hockey goalkeeper.

Liverpool 1920-21 season. The side finished fourth in the First Division.

up spot above Burnley and Chelsea. In the FA Cup that season Liverpool reached the quarter-finals with wins over South Shields, Luton and Birmingham before they lost 2-1 at Huddersfield. The following season they reached fourth again — this time only eight points adrift of the new champions Burnley — but their FA Cup run ended in the second round. A win over Manchester United was quickly followed by a 1-0 defeat at St James's Park, Newcastle. Again the playing staff was increased and Liverpool signed two Merseyside brothers called Wadsworth. Harold was a left-winger and Walter, a centre half.

The first match of 1921-2 gave Liverpool fans little hope that by the end of the campaign their team would have carried off the First Division Championship when Sunderland beat the Anfield club 3-0 at Roker Park. But Liverpool soon 'got it right' and soon their defence was proving as rock-like as any in the First Division. The Sunderland defeat was followed by a run of wins, and even a lapse at the end of the season, when Liverpool won only a point a game from their last seven, failed to stop them taking the title. League matches now numbered forty-two but Liverpool had the marvellous defensive record of only thirty-six goals against, with sixty-three goals 'for' being shared by Harry Chambers, Tommy Miller, Dick Forshaw and the rest of the Liverpool forward line. In the FA Cup, Liverpool shattered Sunderland 5-0 in the first round after a 1-1 draw at Roker Park to avenge the league defeat, but in the next round West Brom won 1-0 at Anfield.

Six points clear of Tottenham Hostpur, the runners up of 1921-2, Liverpool did even better when they retained the title in the following season. Although the margin over the runners-up — this time, Sunderland — was the same, Liverpool had scored sixty points to equal West Brom's record set three seasons earlier. Liverpool lost only one game at Anfield and conceded only thirty-one goals, with seventy going into opponent's nets. Thus, Elisha Scott had let in only sixty-seven goals in two full seasons of First Division goalkeeping. The Irishman was to make 429 appearances for Liverpool in League games and win thirty Irish caps — the last four with Belfast Celtic.

Liverpool started that second championship season in tremendous fashion, winning their first five home games and beating Everton 5-1 into the bargain — a result which would have made John Houlding smile wryly to himself. Another incident worthy of mention in that historic season was a goal scored by Liverpool's outside left, Fred Hopkin, although the thought of Hopkin scoring at all is something of a revelation when the record books show that in well over 300 league matches for Liverpool, he only found the back of the net nine times. But of those nine, this one was his first and most spectacular, although not in the way you might imagine. Hopkin opened his small account with a goal against Bolton Wanderers who were then on their way to the first-ever Wembley FA Cup Final in 1923. The factor which singles out Hopkins goal is that it was immediately followed by a fire in one of the Anfield grandstands. Perhaps it was as well that he scored precious few more! Liverpool went from the end of December to the beginning of March that season without conceding a goal in

Trainer Charlie Wilson holds the League Championship trophy while player Andy McGuigan looks on during the Championship procession of 1922.

Liverpool's two consecutive First Division titles were won like this:

1921-2 Season

	P	W	D	L	F	A	Pts
1 Liverpool	42	22	13	7	63	36	57
2 Tottenham	42	21	9	12	65	39	51
3 Burnley	42	22	5	15	72	54	49
4 Cardiff	42	19	10	13	61	53	48

1922-3 Season

	P	W	D	L	F	A	Pts
1 Liverpool	42	26	8	8	70	31	60
2 Sunderland	42	22	10	10	72	54	54
3 Huddersfield	42	21	11	10	60	32	53
4 Newcastle	42	18	12	12	45	37	48

The players who took the Reds to the First Division titles of 1921-2 and 1922-3 were: Scott, Longworth, McKinlay, Lucas, McNab, Wadsworth (W), Bromilow, Lacey, Forshaw, Lewis, Shone, Chambers, Hopkin, Johnson.

The Liverpool playing staff and directors pose with the League Championship trophy before the start of the 1922-3 season. It was to stay at Anfield for another year.

eight First Division matches and there was no doubt that the Championship was going to Anfield for the fourth time.

In the FA Cup, Liverpool reached the third round with a 4-1 win at Arsenal's Highbury after the sides had drawn 0-0 at Anfield, and a 2-0 win at Wolverhampton before Sheffield United put paid to any thoughts that Liverpool may have been entertaining of a League and Cup 'double'. United came to Liverpool and won 2-1. Thus relieved, Liverpool stormed away with the title.

In the four seasons since the end of World War I, Liverpool had played 168 First Division matches and scored 255 goals, with only 146 against. They had won eighty-five matches and lost only thirty-seven. For a team which spent the last two pre-war seasons more concerned with staying away from the foot of the table, it was a splendid record, even allowing for the sweeping changes that the war brought to most clubs. Liverpool's manager, Tom Watson, sadly died in 1920 before he could see the end results of his team building, and the side which went to the two Championships was managed by David Ashworth. Ashworth's successes did not keep him at Anfield, however, and he soon moved on to Oldham Athletic as team boss. His replacement as Liverpool manager was a name from the club's very beginnings. Matt McQueen had played in the very first Liverpool team and his contribution to the game in general, as well as to Liverpool Football Club in particular, was great. Between being a Liverpool player, manager and director, McQueen even found time to qualify as a Football League referee.

Liverpool 1925-6. The side which finished seventh in the First Division.

Jimmy 'The Parson' Jackson shaking hands with Hunter Hart of Everton before a match at Anfield.

But between the winning of the title in 1922-3 and the outbreak of another war in 1939 Liverpool's name did not appear on a single trophy. The Reds were to experience one of those lean spells which all football clubs endure from time to time. In contrast, Everton won the First Division title in 1927-8, 1931-2 and 1938-9; the FA Cup in 1933 and even the Second Division Championship in 1930-1, although, astonishingly, Liverpool still managed to finish above their Merseyside rivals eleven times during that period.

The writing was on the wall for Liverpool in the season after their second triumph. At a time when they might have been challenging for a hat-trick of First Division titles, they slipped to twelfth place in the table while Huddersfield took the championship — ironically, to start themselves off on the road to three successive First Division titles. Liverpool conceded only forty-eight goals, but in turn, managed to score only forty-nine and it was this lack of finishing power which was to blame for their years in the First Division wilderness. In the FA Cup of 1923-4, Liverpool reached the last eight by beating Bradford City, Bolton Wanderers and Southampton, before Newcastle won their fourth round clash, 1-0 at St James's Park.

Clearly, more new players had to be found, particularly goalscorers, and McQueen was soon busy in the transfer market. His most significant signing was a man destined to become part of the Liverpool legend. Gordon Hodgson was a South African and a member of that country's touring party when he decided to stay in England in 1926. He joined Liverpool and made an immediate impact with sixteen goals in the 1926-7 season. They were to be the first of many. By the time he left the Reds for Aston Villa ten years later, Hodgson had scored 233 goals in 358 Football League matches for Liverpool, a record which stood for many seasons. Liverpool also benefited from a freak incident in a First Division match at Villa Park in 1927-8 when their captain, Don McKinlay, was injured and made an on-the-field decision to move Jimmy McDougall, an inside-forward, back to wing-half. McDougall took the new position like the proverbial duck to water and played there for the next ten seasons, winning two Scottish caps into the bargain.

As Liverpool moved into the 1930s, the famous Spion Kop was rebuilt in its more familiar style of

> Liverpool signed Jimmy 'Parson' Jackson, a full-back from Aberdeen, in 1926. Jackson was ordained in 1933 and became one of the very few Football League professionals to become a clergyman.

A pre-season practice match in progress at Anfield on 20 August 1929.

> *Liverpool's South African Gordon Hodgson, besides winning three England caps, also played cricket for Lancashire. He was born in Johannesburg and came to this country with a South African touring team.*

today and there were more comings and goings at Anfield. The club started the new decade by finishing twelfth in the First Division of 1929-30 and being knocked out of the FA Cup in the third round, at home to Second Division Cardiff City (the First and Second Division clubs now came into the Cup at the third round, the format which is used today). It was a fairly depressing time for the Liverpool fans and they said goodbye to several old faces from the 1920s, although they were rapidly being replaced by the inevitable Scots and a whole host of South Africans, so great an impact had the Springbok Hodgson made. One of the Scottish imports was a giant centre-half called Tom Bradshaw who signed from Bury. Bradshaw had played in the Scottish 'Wembley Wizards' side of 1928 which had defeated England 5-1 on their home ground — the side which included Hughie Gallacher and Alec James.

Bradshaw played a memorable part in the Liverpool defeat of Everton in the third round of the 1931-2 FA Cup. The game at Goodison Park was less than one minute old when Dixie Dean put Everton in front before nearly 60,000 fans. But Bradshaw marshalled the Liverpool defence and soon the whole team had settled down and recovered from that sensational start to win 2-1. That season saw Liverpool into the last eight of the FA Cup for the last time until after World War II. After beating Everton, Liverpool went on to victories over Chesterfield and Grimsby Town before they fell at home to Chelsea in the sixth round. That season they hovered around halfway in the First Division and finally finished tenth.

The following season was again a mediocre affair so far as Liverpool was concerned. The only relief from finishing fourteenth in the league was a 7-4 win over Everton at Anfield when Harold Barton scored four times. But Everton were to finish slightly above Liverpool in 1932-3 and they also went on to win the FA Cup, beating Manchester City 3-0 at Wembley after Liverpool had gone tumbling out at West Bromwich Albion in the third round. In the meantime, a new player was making his way into the Liverpool first team. Berry Nieuwenheys was one of the South Africans signed in the wake of Hodgson's goalscoring feats and he brought a new dimension to the art of wing-play. Loping up the left-hand touchline like the Springbok he was, Nieuwenheys troubled opposing defences with his deceptive speed and fine shot.

England international wing-half Tommy Bromilow holds Anfield's lucky black cat. Bromilow won five caps between 1921 and 1926.

Liverpool players persuaded to do a 'Wembley Walk' for the local press in 1929. But the club's next FA Cup Final appearance would not be until 1950.

In 1933-4 Liverpool were struggling against relegation for part of the season. Eventually they finished in eighteenth place, but just four fewer points would have seen them drop into the Second Division. In the FA Cup Bolton Wanderers won 3-0 at Anfield in the fifth round after Liverpool played one of their rare matches against the 'forgotten' team of Merseyside, Tranmere Rovers and beat them 3-1 at Anfield in the previous round. With eighty-seven goals conceded, Liverpool knew that the defence must be strengthened. The following season this was underlined. Although Liverpool managed to finish seventh in the table — thanks to the goalscoring powers of Hodgson and company — they conceded eighty-eight goals, making 175 against in just two seasons.

Even allowing for the fact that Everton had also let in eighty-eight goals in finishing one place below

Liverpool in 1934-5, the Anfield management was now keen to sign the very best and where better to look than at the England team? England's full-backs at that time were Derby County's Tommy Cooper and Sheffield Wednesday's Ernie Blenkinsop. Cooper was a deadly placer of the ball and Blenkinsop's uncanny positioning made them the ideal targets. Soon they had exchanged the white of Derby and the blue and white of Wednesday for the blood-red shirt of Liverpool and in 1935-6, the Reds conceded twenty-four fewer goals than the previous season. The drawback to this vast improvement was that, at the other end of the scale, Liverpool had also scored twenty-five fewer and the net result was that they finished the season in nineteenth place, missing relegation by only three points. Football is indeeed a fickle mistress!

New signings were still finding their way to Anfield, although not all of them were a roaring success. In 1935, for instance, Liverpool signed Tom Johnson, an inside-forward who had already won five England caps with Manchester City and Everton, although by this time, he was playing in the Third Division North with Barrow. In less than forty matches for Liverpool Johnson managed to score only eight goals and was soon on his way. Gordon Hodgson left for Aston Villa for less than £5,000, after winning three England caps while at Anfield and Stockport County's Fred Howe succeeded him as the man most likely to score goals.

Liverpool's new manager was George Kay, the man who had captained West Ham United in the famous 'White Horse' FA Cup Final of 1923 and he brought in players to give Liverpool's attack its teeth once more, although again there were failures. Ted Harston had scored fifty-odd goals for Mansfield Town and yet he could not find his feet in the First Division. Netting goals in the Third Division was one thing, but beating the top defences in the country was another and Harston played only half a dozen games in the First Division. There were success stories also. Nineteen-year-old Bill Fagan was signed from Preston North End and did well for Liverpool; so did Phil Taylor who joined the Anfield club from Third Division Bristol Rovers.

But Liverpool's most famous signing of those inter-war years was none other than Matt Busby. Busby joined Liverpool from Manchester City midway through the 1935-6 season. He had won an FA Cup-winners medal and just a single Scottish cap with Manchester City as a right-half. When he came to Anfield he had played over 200 league games for City and he went on to play over 100 for Liverpool, including all forty-two in the final season before the start of World War II. Busby was a talented wing-half but, of course, his name became legendary, only when he took over the reins of bombed out Manchester United after the war. His career at

Sam English who, despite the name, won two caps for Ireland. English came to Anfield in 1933 and scored 18 goals in 28 games before moving on.

Liverpool added nothing to the few honours which he had won as a player. Liverpool never finished higher than eleventh during his four seasons at Anfield and in the FA Cup, their best was a fifth round appearance in the 1937-8 season when Huddersfield won 1-0 at Anfield en route for the Wembley final.

Liverpool's 1939-40 season was only one week long as Germany invaded Poland and football was once again suspended. But there were already on the club's books, some of the players who would form the nucleus of the side which would win the First Division championship when football started up again after the war. Four players were forwards — Billy Liddell, Cyril Done, Jack Balmer and Bill Fagan — and Liddell in particular was to become

Liverpool 1937-8. Back row left to right: Browning, Bush, Busby, Riley, Taylor, Harley, Dabbs. Front row: Nieuwenhuys, Shafto, Cooper, Fagan, Rogers, Hanson.

Liverpool 1938-9. Back row left to right: Bush, Busby, Taylor, Riley, G. Wilson (trainer), Rogers, Harley, G. H. Richards (director). Front row: Nieuwenhuys, Balmer, Cooper, W. J. Harropp (chairman), McInnes, Fagan, Van Den Berg. Tommy Cooper was signed from Derby, but was tragically killed during World War II.

one of the most respected and famous players in the history of the Football League. Liddell signed for Liverpool from a Scottish junior club called Lochgelly Violet towards the end of the 1938-9 season as a seventeen-year-old boy from Dunfermline. Although he had to wait until 1946-7 to make his First Division debut for Liverpool, Liddell soon began to make a name for himself in the sometimes topsy-turvey world of war-time regional football. In only his second game in a Liverpool first team shirt, he scored a hat-trick against Manchester City — Frank Swift and all — and in 1942 he was 'capped' by Scotland in a team which included Bill Shankly, Matt Busby and Jock Dodds.

Cyril Done had already scored his first 'official' goal for Liverpool with a shot on the last Saturday of peace in 1939. Done hailed from Bootle and at six feet in height and well-built he packed a powerful shot; Jack Balmer had more experience. He had signed for Liverpool after a few games with Everton as an amateur and in his first season of 1935-6 he had scored eight times.

PEACE — AND THE CHAMPIONSHIP

The FA Cup of 1945-6 — the Football League did not resume operations until the following season — was a strange, unwieldy affair with two-legged ties from the very first rounds and Liverpool found themselves involved in two third round matches with Third Division Chester, which they won 2-0 and 2-1. But in the fourth round Liverpool travelled to Burnden Park for the first-leg and were hammered 5-0. Although they won the return match, Liverpool could only manage two goals and had to wait another season before they could launch themselves on another trophy. Liddell missed Liverpool's summer tour of Canada because he was still serving as a navigator in the RAF; but when he finally made his First Division debut against Chelsea, he helped Liverpool to a 7-4 win and the Reds were on the way to becoming the first League champions of another new era.

Liverpool's new chairman Billy McConnell was responsible for the signing of centre-forward Albert Stubbins, who he whisked from Newcastle United for £12,000, despite keen interest shown by rivals Everton; and with the forward line now complete, Liverpool's new signing scored as they beat Bolton 3-1 at Burnden Park — revenge for the FA Cup humiliation of the previous season and a result which put Liverpool on the road to a twelve-match unbeaten run. But although Stubbins was finding the net regularly, Jack Balmer created a piece of history by becoming the first player ever to score three successive hat-tricks. They were scored in November 1946 against Portsmouth, Derby (away) and Arsenal and even though Denis Westcott of Wolves scored four against Liverpool at Anfield as Wolves won 5-1, Balmer's goals were another sure sign of Liverpool's supremacy. But the winter of 1946-7 was an appalling one and soon the Anfield club had a backlog of fixtures — a problem not helped by their run in the FA Cup when they reached the semi-finals.

The cup was back to normal after its two-legged approach of the previous season and in the third round Liverpool beat Walsall 5-2 at Fellows Park; Grimsby Town and Derby County were the Reds' next victims and then they faced Birmingham City in the sixth round at Anfield. The score was 1-1 when Liddell crossed low and hard and Stubbins hurled himself forward to head past a helpless Birmingham goalkeeper to make the score 2-1. Liverpool finished 4-1 winners and Stubbins netted himself a hat-trick. The semi-final was against Burnley at Ewood Park, Blackburn, but neither side could break the deadlock in a goalless draw and another attempt was made to resolve the matter of who would meet Charlton Athletic in the final at

Liverpool 1946-7. The first Football League season after the war and Liverpool stormed straight to the First Division title.

> *Liverpool full-back Jim Harley, a member of the 1946-7 championship squad, won Glasgow's Powderhall Sprint under the assumed name of A.B. Mitchell when he was eighteen.*

Wembley — Charlton had beaten Newcastle United 4-0 at Leeds — when Burnley and Liverpool replayed at Maine Road. Again, Liverpool found goals hard to come by and after ninety minutes Burnley were through to Wembley with a lone goal scored by Ray Harrison.

The bad winter meant that the Football League season dragged on into June and with seven matches to play — and only two of them at Anfield — Liverpool were nine points behind Wolves. The championship was as tight as any and in the end Liverpool's incredible run of thirteen points from the last fourteen available gave them the title over Manchester United, Wolves and Stoke. Wolves had managed only one point and Stoke had fallen at the last hurdle, losing their match at Sheffield United 2-1, when a win would have put them level with Liverpool and given them the title on goal average. Manchester United, managed by Matt Busby who had turned down a Liverpool coaching job, were the eventual runners-up.

Liverpool's last match had been at Wolverhampton Wanderers — who themselves would have taken the title with a win over the Reds — and the ever

reliable Stubbins and Balmer had scored the goals which gave Liverpool a 2-1 win, although Billy Liddell found himself battling away at the heart of the Liverpool defence as Wolves tried to regain control of the game. After the longest season on record, Liverpool were the champions, though not daring to celebrate until news of Stoke's defeat filtered through from Bramall Lane.

Liverpool used twenty-six players that season — quite a high number for a successful side — including a young wing-half from Durham called Bob Paisley who won a place late in the season. They had averaged two goals a game and their leading scorers were Balmer and Stubbins, each with twenty-four goals. Liverpool had lost five

Liverpool striker Albert Stubbins has the additional honour of being the favourite footballer of that other famous Liverpool performer, ex-Beatle Paul McCartney!

games at Anfield and five away from home in reaching the top. They had conceded fifty-two goals with a defence built around Welsh international goalkeeper Cyril Sidlow and half-backs, Phil Taylor, Bill Jones and Laurie Hughes, not forgetting right-back Ray Lambert who signed for Liverpool while still a schoolboy and who won five Welsh international caps. On the sidelines just waiting for a chance of an extended run in the Liverpool team were many talented youngsters and as the long, cold winter of 1946-7 gave way to one of the best summers in living memory, Liverpool were, no doubt,

looking forward to the coming season and another attempt at taking the First Division title for the second successive year.

Liverpool's 1946-7 First Division Championship side was: Sidlow; Lambert, Harley, Ramsden; Taylor, Jones (W.H.), Hughes, Paisley; Watkinson, Balmer, Stubbins, Done, Fagan, Liddell. The top of the table looked like this:

	P	W	D	L	F	A	Pts
1 Liverpool	42	25	7	10	84	52	57
2 Man Utd	42	22	12	8	95	54	56
3 Wolves	42	25	6	11	98	56	56
4 Stoke	42	24	7	11	90	53	55

Far from notching up another championship win, Liverpool fell away so badly in 1947-8 that they finished in eleventh place in the First Division, caught up in a golden age of football when there were so many excellent players and clubs. Arsenal won the League Championship with Manchester United again just failing, and having to be content with runner-up spot. Liddell, who had played for Great Britain against the Rest of Europe the previous season, was one of those 'greats' and wherever the Scottish international played he drew the applause and cheers of the crowd.

There were several highspots in the season, despite Liverpool's disappointing league form, and despite their fourth round FA Cup defeat at the hand of Manchester United who won 3-0 at, of all places, Goodison Park (United's Old Trafford was still out of commission following the war and they shared Maine Road with Manchester City, who on that day were at home to Chelsea). No doubt, the best thing to happen that season, so far as Liverpool fans were concerned, was the 'double' over Everton. Liverpool won 4-0 at Anfield and 3-0 at Goodison Park and as Everton finished three places below Liverpool, we can assume that there were some satisfied faces at Anfield. In addition, Liverpool attracted a record gate of almost 45,000 spectators for a friendly match at Newcastle United on St Valentine's Day 1948, to underline that although they had fallen from the very top of the tree, they were still looked upon as one of the most exciting and entertaining teams in the land.

In the 1948-9 season Liverpool were again mid-table, finishing in twelfth place while Portsmouth took the First Division title. The Reds won thirteen and lost fifteen of their forty-two league matches

The end of a 10-month season. May 31, 1947 and Jack Balmer and Stan Cullis shake hands before the match that decided the First Division title. Wolves had to win to lift the championship but it was Liverpool who triumphed 2-1 to bring the title to Anfield.

and in the FA Cup they reached the fifth round before Wolves beat them 3-1 at Molineux. But FA Cup glory was just around the corner, although not many Liverpool fans could remember the club's last — and at the time, only — FA Cup Final appearance, way back in 1914.

In 1949-50 Liverpool reached Wembley for the first time. Their cup run started quietly enough with a goalless draw at Blackburn Rovers before Liverpool won the replay at Anfield 2-1; Exeter City at home and Stockport County away, gave Liverpool an easy passage to the sixth round and a home game with Stanley Matthews's Blackpool. Liverpool won 2-1 and the semi-final draw set all Merseyside alight — Liverpool would meet Everton at Maine Road on Grand National Day! Like almost all occasions which promise so much, the all-Merseyside semi-final failed to live up to its pre-match billing. Perhaps the occasion overawed the players. At any rate, Liverpool won 2-0, the goals coming either side of half-time. First, Paisley chipped the ball into

Billy Liddell scored a spectacular goal against Portsmouth in a First Division match when he headed home from well outside the penalty area in 1948-9, the season that Portsmouth won the championship.

the Everton penalty area and Liddell put the Everton goalkeeper, George Burnett, in two minds as he screamed into the area. Burnett grabbed clumsily at the ball and could only help it over the line to put Liverpool ahead; in the second half, another tangle in the Everton defence gave Liddell a half-chance. Liddell seemed the one player on the field who was completely unaffected by nerves and he tucked the ball comfortably home from the narrowest of angles.

Meanwhile, Arsenal and Chelsea had been drawing 2-2 at White Hart Lane. The replay was also on Spurs ground and this time Arsenal won 1-0 with players of the calibre of George Swindin, Laurie Scott, Wally Barnes, Leslie Compton, Alex Forbes, Joe Mercer, Denis Compton, Reg Lewis and Jimmy Logie. That Arsenal side was one of the finest ever produced at Highbury, eclipsing even the team which won the League and Cup 'double' in 1971.

Liverpool 1949-50. Back row left to right: George Kay (manager), Taylor, Lambert, Sidlow, Paisley, Spicer, A. Shelley (trainer). Front row: Payne, Baron, Stubbins, Fagan, Liddell, Hughes. Ten of the players appeared in the FA Cup Final in 1950. The unlucky man was Bob Paisley who was replaced by Bill Jones.

The immediate problem for Liverpool was the Arsenal captain Joe Mercer. Since being transferred to the Gunners some six years earlier from Everton, Mercer had continued to live in Hoylake and was allowed to train at Anfield. Now that he faced Liverpool in the FA Cup Final, Mercer found himself training alone when Anfield was deserted. Naturally, Liverpool could not afford to have a 'spy' in their camp. Another problem was that both sides played in red shirts and although today, only one team changes, in 1950 both Liverpool and Arsenal found themselves running out at Wembley in unfamiliar colours. Liverpool wore white shirts with red collars and cuffs and black shorts; Arsenal played in a most attractive gold and white strip. The customary pre-match rituals were followed with Liverpool spending the eve of the final at a Weybridge hotel, although Arsenal chose to lunch in the familiar portals of Highbury, Tom Whittaker, their manager, no doubt hoping that some of the inspiration of the great Herbert Chapman would rub off on his team. A torrential downpour saturated the Wembley pitch and did much to dampen the fervour of the crowd when both teams were introduced to King George VI.

After seventeen minutes Liverpool were a goal down when Arsenal scored what Tony Pawson in his *100 Years of the FA Cup* described as 'a goal fit to set before a king'. Swinden found Denis Compton with a long throw and the centre-half headed it on to Barnes. With Cox breaking down the right, the Liverpool defence looked to Barnes to swing the ball to him but instead the full-back played a long through ball to where Logie had run down the centre of the field. Arsenal's centre-forward Goring raced across the face of Liverpool's defence, drawing out Hughes, and Lewis stroked the ball into the vacant space and the path of Reg Lewis. Sidlow had no chance and just before the goalkeeper reached Lewis, the Arsenal man slipped the ball past him and into the empty net. It was a goal of glorious construction and execution, worthy of any great occasion.

Three minutes after half-time Liverpool might have drawn level when Liddell — who had suffered some tough treatment from Forbes and Scott — crossed high into Swinden's box and the Arsenal goalkeeper could only palm the ball out to where Payne was rushing in. The Liverpool right-winger headed back towards Arsenal's goal and what appeared an empty net but only managed to place the ball into the arms of the grateful Swinden. In the seventeenth minute of the second half — the same stage at which Liverpool had conceded their first-half goal — Arsenal went 2-0 ahead. It was Lewis again who inflicted the damage, running on to a classic flick from Cox before running the ball past Sidlow to put the result of the game beyond doubt.

Liverpool could hardly complain. They had taken on one of the best attacks in the land and had failed to hold its inventive genius. The Reds defence had a consistently shaky look about it and the wing-halves and inside-forwards failed to serve up anything for the forwards to use.

> *Liverpool's team for the 1949-50 FA Cup Final against Arsenal at Wembley was: Sidlow; Lambert, Spicer; Taylor, Hughes, Jones; Payne, Baron, Stubbins, Fagan, Liddell. Stubbins later became a journalist in his native North-East.*

Manager George Kay's team selection has been drawn into question when he left out Bob Paisley in favour of Bill Jones, and allowed Kevin Baron to retain his place in favour of the now-fit Jack Balmer. But the fact remains that Arsenal were a fine side and would probably have beaten Liverpool eight times out of ten that season, although the First Division honours had been exclusively Liverpool's with a 2-0 win at Anfield and a 2-1 win at Highbury. Perhaps those victories were the two which Liverpool were meant to take!

It was those four points against Arsenal in the league which helped Liverpool into a position where they were at one time challenging for the League and Cup 'double' in 1949-50. They did not lose a league match until the twentieth game of the season, but faded badly and at the end were five points behind champions Portsmouth — who had taken the title for the second successive season. Those five points were enough to send Liverpool into eventual eighth place in the First Division behind Pompey, Wolves, Sunderland, Manchester United, Newcastle, Arsenal and Blackpool. The Reds suffered a heavy 5-1 defeat at the hand of Newcastle United when they visited St James's Park and altogether Liverpool conceded fifty-four goals and scored ten more.

The 1949-50 season began something of a watershed in the affairs of Liverpool Football Club. The side had been members of the First Division since 1905 — a run of thirty-five consecutive seasons in the best league in the world, discounting the war years. The famous red shirts of Liverpool would have to suffer a period of darkness before they once again lit a torch on Merseyside.

Three post-war Liverpool strikers of different eras, showing the evolution of soccer kit from the cumbersome wear of earlier times to the present day lightweight strip of Continental design.

◀ *Cyril Done, seen here in a clash with Derby's Ken Oliver, scored his first goal for Liverpool in 1939 and proved to be a valuable asset in the years after World War Two.*

▲ *Roger Hunt terrorised defences with his ability to be in the right place at the right time to poach goals galore during the 1960s.*

◀ *Kevin Keegan, the superstar who electrified the 1970s.*

1950-1

When Liverpool reached the FA Cup Final in the first year of the 'fifties, Anfield fans might have been forgiven for thinking that the new decade heralded another successful era in the affairs of their beloved club. But the opposite was the case. Liverpool Football Club was on a slippery slope and there was little they could do to maintain their precious hold on the First Division. In 1950-1 the glory days of Liverpool were still years away. There was no European Cup — the competition would not start for another five years — and no Football League Cup. There was no floodlit football and no million-pound stars earning vast fortunes. Crowds, which had been booming in the immediate post-war years of soccer-starved Britain, were falling off in number. This was the scene in which Liverpool's fortunes were set thirty years ago. Incidentally, Liverpool's Lancashire neighbours, New Brighton, were voted out of the Football League that season after finishing bottom of the Third Division (North), with Workington taking their place, although Workington, too, were one day to feel the axe.

Liverpool finished ninth in the First Division, but several players had endured a poor campaign and only Billy Liddell could look back at 1950-1 with any degree of personal satisfaction. Albert Stubbins, so often a stalwart of the Liverpool attack, played in twenty-three Football League matches but could manage only six goals; and

The Wolves defence foils Jimmy Payne at Anfield in December 1950.

Balmer, Fagan and Baron all felt the cold wind of a lean spell. In all Liverpool managed only fifty-three goals — only four clubs scored fewer, including bottom club Everton. In addition, Liverpool had concede fifty-nine, including four in ten minutes when Newcastle United won a First Division match at Anfield — a game which saw Welsh international goalkeeper Cyril Sidlow dropped from the Reds defence. Liverpool's defensive problems were not helped by the fact that centre-half Laurie Hughes had missed the entire season, following an injury.

At Anfield, valuable points were dropped. Bolton were allowed to draw 3-3 and Aston Villa, Middlesbrough, Stoke and West Bromwich Albion also found Liverpool the ideal place for a draw. The bitterest pill to swallow for Liverpool's fans was the 2-0 defeat at the hands of Everton who were on their way to being relegated, although Liverpool did reverse the result when the teams met at Goodison Park. Wolves won 4-1 at Anfield, and Huddersfield, too, scored a 4-1 victory there, although they were to narrowly miss joining Everton in the Second Division. Yet Liverpool scored some good away wins. They went to Fratton Park and completed the 'double' over 1949-50 champions Portsmouth, winning 3-1 on the south coast; and they won at Highbury, although Arsenal were also to finish well above Liverpool. Stoke and Derby were other happier hunting grounds for a Liverpool team slipping slowly from grace.

In the FA Cup Liverpool got no further than the third round. They travelled to Carrow Road and

Liverpool 1950-1. Back row left to right: George Kay (manager), Jones, Lambert, Sidlow, A. Shelley (trainer), Hughes, Spicer. Front row: Liddell, Balmer, Taylor, Fagan, Paisley, Brierley.

what, on paper at least, was an easy tie against Norwich City. The Canaries were pushing Nottingham Forest hard for a place in the Second Division, but they were still a Third Division side. Norwich showed all the cup-fighting inspiration which was to make them famous a few years hence and Liverpool were tabbed 3-1 — a humiliating defeat.

The season had been one of ups and downs, like the affairs of so many good sides whose players are growing collectively past their prime. The defeats were caused by this ageing process; the occasional fine win was the result of these excellent performers still finding that, just now and again, skill will win, despite advancing years. Several of the players were, after all, at Anfield before or during the war which had bitten hard into so many of their careers. Liverpool drew little comfort from their ninth position in 1950-1 — it was a sign of decay, not improvement.

First Division results 1950-1

	H	A
Arsenal	1-3	2-1
Aston Villa	0-0	1-1
Blackpool	1-0	0-3
Bolton	3-3	1-2
Burnley	1-0	1-1
Charlton	1-0	0-1
Chelsea	1-0	0-1
Derby	1-0	2-1
Everton	0-2	3-1
Fulham	2-0	1-2
Huddersfield	1-4	2-2
Man United	2-1	0-1
Middlesbrough	0-0	1-1
Newcastle	2-4	1-1
Portsmouth	2-1	3-1
Sheffield Wed	2-1	1-4
Stoke	0-0	3-2
Sunderland	4-0	1-2
Tottenham	2-1	1-3
West Brom	1-1	1-1
Wolves	1-4	0-2

Final League Record

P	W	D	L	F	A	Pts	Pos
42	16	11	15	53	59	43	9th

FA Cup

Rnd 3   Norwich City   (a)   1-3

1951-2

Liverpool's troubles began early when Eddie Spicer, the man who played left-back in the FA Cup Final of 1950, broke his leg on a close season tour to Sweden. Add to this the fact that Albert Stubbins suffered a thigh injury which resulted in the goalscorer having an operation, and that Laurie Hughes and Phil Taylor both missed twenty-odd matches with knee injuries, then one can see why Liverpool's team plans were wrecked from the start. Again, only Billy Liddell had some bright moments, although Charlie Ashcroft, the man who replaced the out-of-favour Sidlow in the Reds goal, did win an England 'B' cap. But the fact that when Wales played the Rest of the United Kingdom in a 75th anniversary game at Ninian Park, Cardiff in December, 1951, Liverpool could not supply one player towards the twenty-two on the field, spoke volumes for the parlous state of the club.

Yet Liverpool managed to finish eleventh, a position which would have satisfied other clubs. But Liverpool are special and eleventh place was another drop down the First Division ladder. As Manchester United took the title — with the help of a 4-0 over Liverpool at Old Trafford — Anfield was a depressing place. Liverpool scored more goals than the previous season, but the Reds defence also conceded more. In all league matches, sixty-one goals were scored past Liverpool's rearguard and although there were several teams with a worse — much worse — defensive record than that, the writing was clearly on the wall for manager Don Welsh, the former Charlton player who was Manchester born and who became a Liverpool favourite in a series of guest appearances. Welsh had replaced George Kay, whose health had forced his retirement in 1951 after fifteen years at Anfield.

Again, Liverpool were dropping silly points at Anfield — an amazing fact for present-day fans to behold, when the Liverpool stadium is such a bastion that one would almost bank one's life savings there! West Bromwich Albion won 5-2 in 1951-2 and Aston Villa, Manchester City, Portsmouth (wins) and Arsenal, Blackpool, Bolton, Charlton, Chelsea, Manchester United, Middlesbrough, Preston, Sunderland, Spurs and Wolves (draws) also gained points there. In fact, Liverpool won only six matches at Anfield — as many as they won away from home, which is again a curious record explained, no doubt, by the ailing fortunes of a team still good enough to turn in the old flash-in-the-pan result. For instance, Liverpool beat Portsmouth 3-1 at Fratton Park, but lost 2-0 to the same team at Anfield; they beat Manchester City 2-1 at Maine Road but lost by the same scoreline when City came to Liverpool; and Chelsea and Spurs both gained points at Anfield and then failed to stop Liverpool winning in London. In all, only Huddersfield and Stoke were beaten both home and away.

In the FA Cup, Liverpool drew newcomers Workington at home. Workington, unlike some of their more illustrious counterparts who came into

Liverpool 1951-2. Back row left to right: Brierley, Liddell, Jones, Ashcroft, Stubbins, Hughes, A. Shelley (trainer). Front row: Paisley, Payne, Taylor, Williams, Parr, Baron.

Derby goalkeeper Ray Middleton punches clear from Billy Liddell at Anfield in September 1951.

the League and won promotion, were not setting the place alight in 1951-2 and they were bottom of the Third Division (North). Yet Liverpool struggled to beat them 1-0, despite home advantage. Even allowing for the unsettling experience of playing a team of far inferior quality, it was a miserable result. In the next round over 61,000 fans packed Anfield for the visit of Wolverhampton Wanderers and Liverpool put on a much better display, possibly their game was raised by the atmosphere, and they won 2-1. In the fifth round Liverpool faced Burnley at Turf Moor where former Liverpool player, Les Shannon, was inspiring the Lancashire club. Shannon played his part in a 2-0 Burnley win and Liverpool's Wembley dreams were over once more. These were lean years, indeed, for the Reds — by this time, far from super.

Liverpool v Chelsea in December 1951. Payne's shot spins out of Robertson's hands.

First Division results 1951-2

	H	A
Arsenal	0-0	0-0
Aston Villa	1-2	0-2
Blackpool	1-1	0-2
Bolton	1-1	1-1
Burnley	3-1	0-0
Charlton	1-1	0-2
Chelsea	1-1	3-1
Derby	2-0	1-1
Fulham	4-0	1-1
Huddersfield	2-1	2-1
Man City	1-2	2-1
Man United	0-0	0-4
Middlesbrough	1-1	3-3
Newcastle	3-0	1-1
Portsmouth	0-2	3-1
Preston	2-2	0-4
Stoke	2-1	2-1
Sunderland	2-2	0-3
Tottenham	1-1	3-2
West Brom	2-5	3-3
Wolves	1-1	1-2

Final League record

P	W	D	L	F	A	Pts	Pos
42	12	19	11	57	61	43	11th

FA Cup

Rnd 3	Workington	(h)	1-0
Rnd 4	Wolves	(h)	2-1
Rnd 5	Burnley	(a)	0-2

1952-3

The Liverpool defence which had been creaking ominously for almost three seasons finally caved in during 1952-3 and only in the last match of the season did Liverpool manage to avoid relegation. But they could only hope to postpone the drop into the Second Division, such was the magnitude of their task in staying afloat. Eighty-two goals against was a defensive record which only two clubs exceeded — though, strangely, neither were relegated — and it was a total shared with Sunderland who managed to finish ninth in the table. Liverpool scraped to seventeenth position after beating Chelsea 2-0 at Anfield on the very last day of the season, thus hauling themselves just two points clear of twenty-first club Stoke City who had a better goal average than the Reds.

Arsenal found Liverpool's defence a particularly happy hunting ground and twice the Gunners thundered five goals past it — their 5-1 win at Anfield leaving the Liverpool supporters shaking their heads in disbelief. Only twice did the Reds manage to keep a clean sheet on opponents grounds — and they won both matches, incidentally, against Manchester City and Sheffield Wednesday — while at home, only four clubs failed to score at Anfield. Even relegated Derby who finished in bottom place managed to steal a point from under the noses of the Kop.

Portsmouth goalkeeper Butler knocks down Payne's shot in the First Division match at Anfield in September 1952.

Albert Stubbins played his last season with the Reds, appearing only four times during the fight to stay in the First Division, and the Liverpool team-sheet had a few new faces — faces which would serve the club well when the time came to rise again. They included names like A'Court, Bimpson and Moran. Louis Bimpson was a big, strong centre-forward who hailed from Burscough; Alan A'Court was an outside-left from Prescot; and Ronnie Moran, a powerful full-back. The trio came into a woefully weak Liverpool team, unlike the combinations which they would play in towards the latter half of their illustrious careers at Anfield. Liverpool also raided the transfer market when they paid Wolverhampton Wanderers around £12,000 for their Irish international, Sammy Smyth, although Smyth had seen his best days and he was not a success at Anfield.

Liverpool's matches were just one depressing struggle after another. There was never one day when Reds supporters could wake up and feel that two points were in the bag — though they could have felt that Liverpool would at least win through to the fourth round of the FA Cup, following news of their third round draw. Liverpool were pulled out of the hat against Gateshead at Redheugh Park. Gateshead were a Third Division (North) side and even allowing for the fact that they were on the fringes of the promotion race which was eventually won by Liverpool's Lancashire neighbours, Oldham Athletic, there were no Liverpool fans who

First Division results 1952-3

	H	A
Arsenal	1-5	3-5
Aston Villa	0-2	0-4
Blackpool	2-2	1-3
Bolton	0-0	2-2
Burnley	1-1	0-2
Cardiff	2-1	0-4
Charlton	1-2	2-3
Chelsea	2-0	0-3
Derby	1-1	2-3
Man City	0-1	2-0
Man United	1-2	1-3
Middlesbrough	4-1	3-2
Newcastle	5-3	2-1
Portsmouth	1-1	1-3
Preston	2-2	1-1
Sheffield Wed	1-0	2-0
Stoke	3-2	1-3
Sunderland	2-0	1-3
Tottenham	2-1	1-3
West Brom	3-0	0-3
Wolves	2-1	0-3

Final League record

P	W	D	L	F	A	Pts	Pos
42	14	8	20	61	82	36	17th

FA Cup

Rnd 3   Gateshead .... (a)   0-1

Louis Bimpson made his debut in 1952-3. ▶

thought that their side faced anything, other than a formality against the Third Division minnows.

But that is not to allow for that strange ingredient which makes the FA Cup so magical. There are no such things as foregone conclusions in the greatest knockout competition in the world and Liverpool's visit to Gateshead was no exception. The Redheugh Park pitch was covered in a sea of mud and many people on the ground, players, officials and spectators, tried hard to recall when they had last seen a playing surface in such diabolical condition. And to add to the problems, a swirling fog descended on the ground, making the art of spectatorship almost as difficult as the art of trying to play football on the glue-pot. Given that scenario, perhaps what happened next was inevitable. Gateshead scored a goal and Liverpool, try as they might, could not force their way back into the game. They even sent poor Bill Jones up into the attack but even his grit and determination failed to break through a resolute Third Division defence which had been bolstered by the gruesome conditions. Liverpool crashed out, beaten ignominiously by a side they would ordinarily have murdered. That result said much for the way that Liverpool's fortunes were heading.

1953-4

Liverpool could not put off the inevitable. The previous season had been a stay of execution and now the Reds were condemned men. It was the blackest season at Anfield for half a century. It was Liverpool's last in the First Division for eight years — and it came with a vengence from the very first kick-off. Liverpool lost their first fourteen away matches, some by quite staggering margins for the First Division. Manchester United won 5-1 at Old Trafford; Charlton beat the Reds 6-0 at the Valley; Portsmouth triumphed 5-1 at Fratton Park; Chelsea crushed them 5-2 at Stamford Bridge; and West Bromwich Albion by the same score at the Hawthorns. They all contributed to a defensive record of ninety-seven goals against, the worst, by far, in the First Division. Things were not helped by Spicer breaking his leg. It was the second time that Spicer had suffered this injury and it proved to be the end of his playing career.

In a desperate bid to avert the impending disaster, Liverpool moved into the transfer market. Watford's goalkeeper, Dave Underwood, and Carlisle United centre-half, Geoff Twentyman, were recruited. Then manager Don Welsh went back to his old club Charlton Athletic for full-back Frank Lock and John Evans, a forward. Another defender made the journey from Old Trafford when Manchester United's full-back Tom McNulty came to Anfield.

Liverpool actually managed to score more goals than they had managed in any season since they won the First Division championship in 1946-7. Louis Bimpson score all four when Liverpool hammered Burnley at Anfield; and Aston Villa were routed 6-1 with Sammy Smyth notching two of the goals; Liverpool also scored four goals each against Sunderland and Middlesbrough and also shared eight goals with Manchester United in a drawn game at Anfield.

But still the goals were going in at the other end and Preston North End won 5-1 at Anfield, just to remind Liverpool fans — if they needed any reminding — that their famous club was about to relinquish its First Division status, held since before World War I. Liverpool managed only nine wins — two of them away from home — and lost twenty-three matches. It was a sorry procession and at the end of the season the foot of the First Division looked like this:

		P	W	D	L	F	A	Pts
16	Tottenham	42	16	5	21	65	76	37
17	Man City	42	14	9	19	62	77	37
18	Sunderland	42	14	8	20	81	89	36
19	Sheff Wed	42	15	6	21	70	91	36
20	Sheff Utd	42	11	11	20	69	90	33
21	Middlesbro	42	10	10	22	60	91	30
22	Liverpool	42	9	10	23	68	97	28

Ted Ditchburn and Alf Ramsey of Spurs hold up a Liverpool attack from A'Court and Anderson in January 1954.

In the FA Cup Liverpool again went out at the first attempt, although the defeat was a little more honourable than the previous season, when they went to Burnden Park, home of First Division Bolton Wanderers, and lost by the only goal of the game. It was Bolton's third win against Liverpool, for they were to beat them twice in the league as well. In the FA Cup match, the goal was scored by England centre-forward, Nat Lofthouse, who must have relished the opportunity to play against a defence which was having such an unhappy time.

The £50,000 which Don Welsh had spent on players had not been able to avert the crisis and to add to Liverpool's humiliation, their Merseyside neighbours, Everton, came back into the First Division when they tied on points with Second Division champions Leicester City and took runners-up spot on goal average, a point ahead of Blackburn Rovers. Liverpool would no longer be visiting Old Trafford and Highbury. The Reds team bus would now be pulling up at the unfashionable Second Division halts of Plymouth, Hull and Doncaster.

◀ *Bimpson scores Liverpool's third goal in their 4-0 win over Burnley in September 1953.*

First Division results 1953-4

	H	A
Arsenal	1-2	0-3
Aston Villa	6-1	1-2
Blackpool	5-2	0-3
Bolton	1-2	0-2
Burnley	4-0	1-1
Cardiff	0-1	1-3
Charlton	2-3	0-6
Chelsea	1-1	2-5
Huddersfield	1-3	0-2
Man City	2-2	2-0
Man United	4-4	1-5
Middlesbrough	4-1	1-0
Newcastle	2-2	0-4
Portsmouth	3-1	1-5
Preston	1-5	1-2
Sheffield Utd	3-0	1-3
Sheffield Wed	2-2	1-1
Sunderland	4-3	2-3
Tottenham	2-2	1-2
West Brom	0-0	2-5
Wolves	1-1	1-2

Final League record

P	W	D	L	F	A	Pts	Pos
42	9	10	23	68	97	28	22nd

FA Cup

Rnd 3 Bolton .... (a) 0-1

1954-5

Ronnie Moran heads clear from a Plymouth attack in September 1954.

The last time that Liverpool had been in the Second Division, Burton United and Glossop North End were amongst the Reds opponents—so it was hardly surprising that there were thousands of Anfield supporters in 1954-5 for whom this was an entirely new experience. Liverpool, of course, had only one thing in mind—to return to the First Division as quickly as possible. But the Reds team was in the throes of change and the whole unit had to come to terms with their new environment. So Liverpool could finish no higher than eleventh place in the table, way behind the promoted clubs, Birmingham City and Luton Town.

In fact, Liverpool were faced with the possibility of a drop into the Third Division (North) at one stage during the season. In December 1954 they travelled to St Andrews and high-riding Birmingham City. The result was the heaviest defeat in the long story of Liverpool. On an ice-rink of a pitch Birmingham skated round the Reds defence to beat them 9-1. It is a picture which Liverpool fans of the 'eighties will find incomprehensible. They would also find it hard to swallow that their beloved club also went crashing 6-1 to Rotherham United at Millmoor during that season, all of which goes to explain how Liverpool managed to concede almost a century of goals. The Reds also scored ninety-two, which was their highest total for half-a-century, and of those, the irrepressible Billy Liddell scored thirty from the centre-forward berth. John Evans scored twenty-nine, including four in the 5-3 win over Bristol Rovers at Anfield.

But Liverpool's defence was incapable of holding out and no matter how many goals the forwards supplied, it always seemed as though Liverpool would concede more. On balance, however, it was an average kind of a season with an equal number of games won and lost and ten matches drawn. Liverpool's turning point came in an FA Cup fourth round tie at Goodison Park. The Reds had struggled against Lincoln City in the third round, drawing 1-1 at Sincil Bank and scraping through with the only goal of the Anfield replay. And with a record ten defeats and two draws in their previous twelve league matches, they went to face Everton without anyone giving them much hope.

Football is a fascinating game and there is no

stronger fascination than the FA Cup — as Liverpool themselves would readily testify after their humiliation at Gateshead two seasons earlier. The Reds stormed into a 2-0 lead against Everton when Billy Liddell evaded a lunging tackle in the Goodison club's penalty area before planting the ball home, and when Alan A'Court added a second shortly afterwards. Trailing by that score at half-time, one can only imagine what was said in the Everton dressing room as the players swallowed their half-time drink. But whatever instructions they had been given, Everton were no match, on that day, for their Merseyside rivals. In the second half John Evans scored twice and Liverpool were home 4-0, despite the fact that Hughes was a passenger for most of the last forty-five minutes due to a knee injury. Billy Liddell dropped back into the midfield and Dave Hickson, Everton's lively striker, could find no way past Twentyman who had established a permanent place for himself in the Liverpool side.

The win was more important to Liverpool than probably any other that season. Although they lost at home to Huddersfield Town in the next round, victory over the old enemy had inspired the Reds to tackle the business of survival and at the end of the Season they had done that comfortably. It was Derby and Ipswich who tumbled into the dark basement of the Third Division, while for Liverpool, the only way from that moment was up.

Second Division results 1954-5

	H	A
Birmingham	2-2	1-9
Blackburn	4-1	3-4
Bristol Rov	5-3	0-3
Bury	1-1	4-3
Derby	2-0	2-3
Doncaster	3-2	1-4
Fulham	4-1	2-1
Hull	2-1	2-2
Ipswich	6-2	0-2
Leeds	2-2	2-2
Lincoln	2-4	3-3
Luton	4-4	2-3
Middlesbrough	3-1	2-1
Notts County	3-1	3-0
Nottm Forest	1-0	1-3
Plymouth	3-3	0-1
Port Vale	1-1	3-4
Rotherham	3-1	1-6
Stoke	2-4	0-2
Swansea	1-1	2-3
West Ham	1-2	3-0

Final League record

P	W	D	L	F	A	Pts	Pos
42	16	10	16	92	96	42	11th

FA Cup

Rnd 3	Lincoln	(a)	1-1
Replay	Lincoln	(h)	1-0
Rnd 4	Everton	(a)	4-0
Rnd 5	Huddersfield	(h)	0-2

Billy Liddell scored 30 goals in 1954-5 and played a big part in Liverpool's great FA Cup win over Everton.

1955-6

Season 1955-6 began a run of incredible near-misses for Liverpool Football Club. Six times they would miss promotion by a whisker before they finally climbed back into the First Division. The improvement which Liverpool had shown in the latter part of the previous season was maintained from the very start of this one. New faces arrived at Anfield and they included Chester's full-back John Molyneux who replaced the faithful Ray Lambert. Lambert had played over 300 Football League games for Liverpool and had been a member of the side which contested the 1950 FA Cup Final against Arsenal. From Liverpool's St Anthony's School came young Jimmy Melia — a man who was to become part of the Anfield success story of the late Fifties and early Sixties. And Scunthorpe United's Dick White joined Liverpool as a centre-half.

Liverpool were on the way back and they showed their intention with some splendid victories, including a 7-0 thrashing of Fulham, a 5-2 win over Nottingham Forest, and a fine 5-0 victory at Barnsley. Liverpool actually scored fewer goals than the previous season but the important factor was that they had also conceded fewer — thirty-three fewer to be exact — and this was the real reason for their vast improvement. The Reds defence had at last settled down and Liverpool fans could again look forward to some performances more in keeping with their famous side.

There was still some way to go, of course, and Liverpool lost sixteen matches, including a 3-0 defeat by Sheffield Wednesday and a 4-0 reverse at the hands of Plymouth who were eventually relegation along with Hull City. At the end of the campaign, these defeats were the difference between Liverpool going back into the First Division at the second attempt and spending another few seasons in the second. They were just four points adrift of the runners up, Leeds United, in a Second Division table which looked like this at the top:

		P	W	D	L	F	A	Pts
1	Sheff Wed	42	21	13	8	101	62	55
2	Leeds	42	23	6	13	80	60	52
3	Liverpool	42	21	6	15	85	63	48
4	Blackburn	42	21	6	15	84	65	48
5	Leicester	42	21	6	15	94	78	48
6	Bristol R	42	21	6	15	84	70	48

◀ *Liverpool's Rudham punches clear from Nottingham Forest's Higham at the City Ground on the opening day of the 1955-6 season. Rudham had a memorable debut as Liverpool won 3-1.*

It could not have been a closer run race and although Sheffield Wednesday were obviously going to be promoted as the season drew to a close, any one of five clubs could have joined them with Leeds finally pulling clear.

Liverpool's season will also be remembered for their FA Cup fifth round replay against Manchester City at Anfield. The Reds had narrowly beaten Third Division club Accrington Stanley and they had to pay two games to dispose of Stanley's bedfellows, Scunthorpe United, before they fought a goalless draw at Maine Road. On a snow-bound Anfield pitch Manchester City took a 2-1 lead in the replay and with the seconds ticking away, fans began to think about their homeward journey when Billy Liddell sprang clear of the City defence and delivered a powerful shot which City's German goalkeeper Bert Trautmann could only watch sail into his net. Liddell wheeled in joy but the referee had blown his whistle as the Scotsman's shot was on its way to goal. Manchester City went on to win the Cup — and, typically, there was no word of complaint from Liddell.

Second Division results 1955-6

	H	A
Barnsley	1-1	5-0
Blackburn	1-2	3-3
Bristol City	2-1	1-2
Bristol Rovers	0-2	2-1
Bury	4-2	4-1
Doncaster	1-2	0-1
Fulham	7-0	1-3
Hull	3-0	2-1
Leeds	1-0	2-4
Leicester	3-1	1-3
Lincoln	2-1	0-2
Middlesbrough	1-1	2-1
Nottm Forest	5-2	3-1
Notts County	2-1	1-2
Plymouth	4-1	0-4
Port Vale	4-1	1-1
Rotherham	2-0	1-0
Sheffield Wed	0-3	1-1
Stoke	2-2	2-3
Swansea	4-1	1-2
West Ham	3-1	0-2

Final League record

P	W	D	L	F	A	Pts	Pos
42	21	6	15	85	63	48	3rd

FA Cup

Rnd 3	Accrington Stanley	(h)	2-0
Rnd 4	Scunthorpe Utd	(h)	3-3
Replay	Scunthorpe Utd	(a)	2-1
Rnd 5	Man City	(a)	0-0
Replay	Man City	(h)	1-2

Liverpool v Leicester, January 1956. Arnell scores Liverpool's second goal from A'Court's pass.

Liverpool 1955-6. Back row left to right: Saunders, McNulty, Lambert, Hughes, Underwood, T. Rowley, Twentyman, Lock, Payne. Front row: A. Rowley, Jackson, Anderson, Bimpson, Evans, Liddell, A'Court.

1956-7

Liverpool inched nearer and nearer to the First Division—this time they were only two points away from rejoining the likes of Arsenal and Manchester United in the top flight. And this time they started the season with a new manager. The Liverpool Board of Directors finally lost patience and decided that a new face was needed if their club was to make that extra-determined leap back to the top. So, Don Welsh found himself without a job and in his place, Liverpool appointed the club's coach, Phil Taylor. Perhaps it was an unfair decision, perhaps not. In football there is no room for near-misses.

More new players arrived, the most famous as far as Liverpool's story is concerned was the Scottish international goalkeeper Tommy Younger, who signed from Hibernian. Younger's signing meant that the Liverpool defensive jigsaw was complete. He was a class goalkeeper and his authority in the penalty area soon ran through the whole side.

Stoke v Liverpool in January 1957. Moran heads the ball for a corner before Coleman can reach it.

Liverpool felt safe with Tommy Younger. Bolton Wanderer's attacking wing-half Johnny Wheeler was another Phil Taylor signing and with the emergence of a new Liverpool, the selectors began to visit Anfield again. Alan A'Court was earmarked as a future England star—though he was not to make his debut until 1958 in the full England side—and Younger maintained his place in the Scotland team. In fact, the former Hibs goalkeeper was a permanent fixture between the Scottish posts during the mid-fifties. To complete Liverpool's list of honours, Ron Moran was selected for the Football League representive team.

Although they finished only one point behind runners-up Nottingham Forest, Liverpool had left themselves too much to do in the last few weeks of the season and even sixteen points from their last ten matches was not a good enough finish to ensure their promotion. They had lost the title earlier with a series of home defeats—they lost four of their ten defeats at Anfield—and away from home any one of ten drawn games might have been won to give them a better springboard for the final assault.

They drew only one match at home when Notts County took a point in a thrilling 3-3 draw. The top of the Second Division finished in this fashion:

		P	W	D	L	F	A	Pts
1	Leicester	42	25	11	6	109	67	61
2	Nottm Forest	42	22	10	10	94	55	54
3	Liverpool	42	21	11	10	82	54	53
4	Blackburn	42	21	10	11	83	75	52
5	Stoke	42	20	8	14	83	58	48
6	Middlesbro	42	19	10	13	84	60	48

Liverpool's debt to Tommy Younger can be seen from that goals against column. It was their lowest since 1950-1. Gerry Byrne, who was also destined to play for England, made his debut at left-back, although he had the unfortunate experience of diverting the ball past Tommy Younger in his very first game in the first team. But he, too, would soon become one of Liverpool's most dependable defenders.

In the FA Cup, however, Liverpool were in for another nasty surprise at the hands of a Third Division club. In the third round they drew Southend United at Roots Hall. Southend were a fair, middle-of-the-table Southern section side but they beat Liverpool 2-1. The ignominy of the defeat was only underlined in the fourth round when Birmingham City took on the giantkillers on the south coast and walloped them 6-1 to show Liverpool that there was nothing to worry about when it came to tackling inferior opposition.

Second Division results 1956-7

	H	A
Barnsley	2-1	1-4
Blackburn	2-3	2-2
Bristol City	2-1	1-2
Bristol Rovers	4-1	0-0
Bury	2-0	2-0
Doncaster	2-1	1-1
Fulham	4-3	2-1
Grimsby	3-2	0-0
Huddersfield	2-3	3-0
Leicester	2-0	2-3
Leyton Orient	1-0	4-0
Lincoln	4-0	3-3
Middlesbrough	1-2	1-1
Nottm Forest	3-1	0-1
Notts County	3-3	1-1
Port Vale	4-1	2-1
Rotherham	4-1	2-2
Sheffield Utd	5-1	0-3
Stoke	0-2	0-1
Swansea	2-0	1-1
West Ham	1-0	1-1

Final League record

P	W	D	L	F	A	Pts	Pos
42	21	11	10	82	54	53	3rd

FA Cup

Rnd 3   Southend .... (a)   1-2

Rowley challenges Rotherham's Ironside in the Second Division match at Anfield in March 1957. Liverpool hammered the Yorkshiremen 4-1.

1957-8

Although Liverpool again failed to win promotion, the 1957-8 season was memorable from several other points of view, including Billy Liddell creating a new record of league appearances, and the switching on of Anfield's floodlights. The only setback to the celebrations was that Liverpool would finish fourth in the Second Division. Liddell made thirty-five appearances in the Second Division, on the way breaking Elisha Scott's record of 429, and he scored twenty-two of Liverpool's seventy-nine league goals. The full glare of the floodlights was officially switched on at the end of October and they signalled the start of another era in the history of the club. In addition to these two events, Phil Taylor signed on two more players — an Evertonian winger called Tony McNamara and Jimmy Harrower, an inside-forward from Tommy Younger's old club Hibernian.

Liverpool's race to the First Division was again thwarted by some poor finishing — the defence held firm again with just fifty-four goals conceded which was one of the best records in the league. But while champions West Ham and third-placed Charlton were scoring a century of goals each (runners-up Blackburn managed ninety-three) Liverpool were one of the poorest scoring sides in the top half of the Second Division.

But silly points were again dropped at home where, although only Middlesbrough managed to win at Anfield, several teams stole a draw, including Barnsley, Huddersfield and West Ham. The Hammers were a good side — championship material — but both the Yorkshire clubs should have been buried on Merseyside. Instead, the points which they took from Liverpool cost them runners-up spot and the Reds actually slipped one place down the table to fourth position. Here is the final Second Division top six for 1957-8:

	P	W	D	L	F	A	Pts
1 West Ham	42	23	11	8	101	54	57
2 Blackburn	42	22	12	8	93	57	56
3 Charlton	42	24	7	11	107	69	55
4 Liverpool	42	22	10	10	79	54	54
5 Fulham	42	20	12	10	97	59	52
6 Sheff Utd	42	21	10	11	75	50	52

There was something missing in the Liverpool make-up. Anfield supporters were still wholly behind their club but at times they must have despaired at the prospect of spending yet another season in the Second Division after so many near misses. And yet the waiting was far from over.

In the FA Cup Liverpool were drawn at home to Southend, the team which had given the Reds some even redder faces twelve months earlier. And when the Third Division outfit held Liverpool to a 1-1 draw at Anfield, Liverpool fans groaned. They need not have worried because Liverpool won the replay at Roots Hall, 3-2, and straight away found themselves with another opponent from the Third Division, Northampton Town. Liverpool beat the Cobblers 3-1 at Anfield and the fifth round draw was kind again when it paired them with Scunthorpe United. Although Scunthorpe won the Third Division (North) that season, Liverpool were not unduly troubled and won 1-0 at the Old Show Ground. There, their luck ran out, however, and First Division-bound Blackburn Rovers won their sixth round match at Ewood Park. Still, it had been a cup run of sorts.

◀ *Southend's Hollis scores at Anfield to set up what might have been the Seasiders' second successive FA Cup shock over Liverpool.*

Second Division results 1957-8

	H	A
Barnsley	1-1	1-2
Blackburn	2-0	3-3
Bristol City	4-3	2-1
Bristol Rovers	2-0	1-3
Cardiff	3-0	1-6
Charlton	3-1	1-5
Derby	2-0	1-2
Doncaster	5-0	1-1
Fulham	2-1	2-2
Grimsby	3-2	1-3
Huddersfield	1-1	1-2
Ipswich	3-1	1-3
Leyton Orient	3-0	0-1
Lincoln	1-0	1-0
Middlesbrough	0-2	2-2
Notts County	4-0	2-0
Rotherham	2-0	2-2
Sheffield Utd	1-0	1-1
Stoke	3-0	2-1
Swansea	4-0	2-0
West Ham	1-1	1-1

Final League record

P	W	D	L	F	A	Pts	Pos
42	22	10	10	79	54	54	4th

FA Cup

Rnd 3	Southend Utd	(h)	1-1
Replay	Southend Utd	(a)	3-2
Rnd 4	Northampton	(h)	3-1
Rnd 5	Scunthorpe Utd	(a)	1-0
Rnd 6	Blackburn	(a)	1-2

Tommy Younger breathes again as this Southend shot whistles past his post. ▼

1958-9

Liverpool's hopes of at last re-instating themselves in the First Division were dashed in the first few weeks of the 1958-9 season. In their first eleven matches the Reds won only ten points and it was a start from which they were never to recover. In the final analysis, Liverpool under Phil Taylor did well to finish as high as fourth again, though this time they were well short of the promoted clubs Sheffield Wednesday and Fulham.

For the first time in his long and illustrious career, Billy Liddell was dropped from the Liverpool team for a reason other than injury, yet despite the fact that he played only nineteen games, Liddell still managed to score fourteen goals — a striking record which would ensure any player a permanent place today, let alone a player of Liddell's calibre.

Taylor ventured into the transfer market again and brought Fred Norris from Mansfield Town to Anfield. Norris was a winger, although his build was not one of a classic wingman. Nevertheless, he was the man to whom Taylor looked to solve his immediate problems. Eventually, Liddell was re-called to the fold over Easter and scored twice in the win over Barnsley to underline that, even at the age of thirty-seven, he could still give Liverpool's attack some sting.

Perhaps the blackest spot in Liverpool's recent history of being giantkilling victims was in the third round of the FA Cup in 1958-9 when they were drawn away to Southern League side Worcester City. Billy Liddell was named as twelfth man for the match and could only watch as his teammates slithered to a sensational 2-1 defeat. That defeat by Worcester City overshadowed Liverpool for the rest of that season. Coupled with the fact that they had lost so much vital ground in the first few weeks, there was little chance of them returning the sort of results that were needed to create a sensational rise to the top of the Second Division and back into the First where their rivals Everton were comfortably placed.

The defence looked a little more creaky than of late and sixty-two goals went past Tommy Younger who was entering his last stages of a career which had been of great service to Liverpool. Conversely, Liverpool found the net eighty-seven times to improve on their previous season's goal tally. But still the points were lost and there was one particularly dark day at Leeds Road, Huddersfield, when Huddersfield Town beat Liverpool 5-0; Town's manager that day was a man called Bill Shankly. Liverpool's overall away record, however, was not that bad. The Reds won nine games away from

Louis Bimpson (left) and Alan Arnell took over the Liverpool attack in 1958-9.

Anfield and drew two to almost give them the point-a-game average that championship sides reckon to take from their away programme. But three games were lost at Anfield and a further three drawn. One of the worst slip-ups was when Liverpool scored three goals against Stoke but allowed the Staffordshire club to bag four goals and both points.

The final Second Division table saw Liverpool well adrift of the top two, thanks to those early season lapses. The top six were:

	P	W	D	L	F	A	Pts
1 Sheff Wed	42	28	6	8	106	48	62
2 Fulham	42	27	6	9	96	61	60
3 Sheff Utd	42	23	7	12	82	48	53
4 Liverpool	42	24	5	13	87	62	53
5 Stoke	42	21	7	14	72	58	49
6 Bristol Rovers	42	18	12	12	80	64	48

There was, however, a rumbling in the hills. A Messiah was coming who would take Liverpool Football Club by the scruff of its neck and breathe life and fire into it until it became one of the world's greatest.

Second Division results 1958-9

	H	A
Barnsley	3-2	2-0
Brighton	5-0	2-2
Bristol City	3-2	3-1
Bristol Rovers	2-1	0-3
Cardiff	1-2	0-3
Charlton	3-0	3-2
Derby	3-0	2-3
Fulham	0-0	1-0
Grimsby	3-3	3-2
Huddersfield	2-2	0-5
Ipswich	3-1	0-2
Leyton Orient	3-0	3-1
Lincoln	3-2	1-2
Middlesbrough	1-2	1-2
Rotherham	4-0	1-0
Scunthorpe	3-0	2-1
Sheffield Utd	2-1	0-2
Sheffield Wed	3-2	0-1
Stoke	3-4	2-0
Sunderland	3-1	1-2
Swansea	4-0	3-3

Final League record

P	W	D	L	F	A	Pts	Pos
42	24	5	13	87	62	53	4th

FA Cup

Rnd 3   Worcester City .... (a)   1-2

Billy Liddell was recalled to the side on Good Friday 1959 and scored twice against Barnsley. Liverpool won 3-2 and completed the double with a 2-0 win at Anfield on Easter Monday.

1959-60

1 December 1959 is one of the most important dates in the story of Liverpool Football Club. That was the day when Bill Shankly came to Anfield. It was the day when the Liverpool story took off into the stars — the day the club was rescued from the dangers of Second Division obscurity by a man who lived, breathed and ate Liverpool football.

That close season had seen the departure of Tommy Younger who went to become player-manager of Falkirk with Bert Slater replacing him in the Liverpool goal. In early November, Phil Taylor made a surprise bid for Everton's centre-forward Dave Hickson and secured the signature of the fiery striker for some £12,000. A few days later, Taylor resigned, admitting that the continual strain of fighting for promotion had left him tired and drained.

Shankly had applied for the Liverpool job before and been turned down when Don Welsh was appointed. But now the Liverpool directors travelled to Huddersfield where Cardiff were playing a Second Division match and soon Shankly was Liverpool's boss. He had been a great wing-half but his managerial record at Carlisle, Grimsby, Workington and Huddersfield was not that impressive. Perhaps he needed Liverpool as much as they needed him. Shankly's first year at Anfield saw two complete teams transferred. Within a month of his arrival, he had made a list of twenty-four players who he did not want and within twelve months they had all departed. His first move into the transfer market was to try and sign Leeds centre-half Jack Charlton but Shankly's offer of £18,000 was turned down and Liverpool felt they could not afford any more cash.

Under Shankly Liverpool finished third in the table and thus missed promotion yet again, this time finishing well behind Aston Villa and Cardiff. Cardiff had won 4-0 at Anfield that season. Two youngsters also made their first league appearances that season. Roger Hunt scored twenty-one goals in thirty-six matches and seventeen-year-old Ian Callaghan came into the side in April. Geoff Twentyman had been released to play for Irish club Ballymena and in his place, Shankly signed Tommy Leishman from Scottish club Hibernian.

In the FA Cup Liverpool beat Leyton Orient 2-1 in the third round but when the fourth round draw saw them matched against Manchester United, even the magic of Shankly could not save his side from a 3-1 defeat at Anfield, although the Reds were not disgraced in defeat by a side in the top six of the First Division.

Liverpool goalkeeper Slater takes the ball from his teammate White and Leyton Orient centre-forward Johnstone at Anfield in November 1959.

Besides running the rule over the Liverpool playing staff, Shankly had also looked long and hard at the coaching staff at Anfield before deciding that people like Joe Fagan, Reuben Bennet and, of course, Bob Paisley, would do exactly the kind of job that he required of them. It was the start of Shankly's Liverpool 'family'. Another face to stay at Anfield was Gerry Byrne. The left-back had been on the transfer list when Shankly arrived but it did not take much of the Shankly presence to persuade Byrne that there was a future for him at Anfield.

Liverpool's latest failure to get out of the Second Division was offset by the fact that everyone could feel the breath of fresh air blowing round the corridors of Anfield. Things were stirring and there were exciting times ahead. The Second Division top six for 1959-60 were:

	P	W	D	L	F	A	Pts
1 Aston Villa	42	25	9	8	89	43	59
2 Cardiff	42	23	12	7	90	62	58
3 Liverpool	42	20	10	12	90	66	50
4 Sheff Utd	42	19	12	11	68	51	50
5 Middlesbrough	42	19	10	13	90	64	48
6 Huddersfield	42	19	9	14	73	52	47

Second Division results 1959-60

Aston Villa	2-1	4-4
Brighton	2-2	2-1
Bristol City	4-2	0-1
Bristol Rovers	4-0	2-0
Cardiff	0-4	2-3
Charlton	2-0	0-3
Derby	4-1	2-1
Huddersfield	2-2	0-1
Hull	5-3	1-0
Ipswich	3-1	1-0
Leyton Orient	4-3	0-2
Lincoln	1-3	2-4
Middlesbrough	1-2	3-3
Plymouth	4-1	1-1
Portsmouth	1-1	1-2
Rotherham	3-0	2-2
Scunthorpe	2-0	1-1
Sheffield Utd	3-0	1-2
Stoke	5-1	1-1
Sunderland	3-0	1-1
Swansea	4-1	4-5

Final League record

P	W	D	L	F	A	Pts	Pos
42	20	10	12	90	66	50	3rd

FA Cup

| Rnd 3 | Leyton Orient | (h) | 2-1 |
| Rnd 4 | Man United | (h) | 1-3 |

Billy Liddell (off picture) gets back among the goals with this one against Stoke City in March 1960. Liverpool won 5-1.

1960-1

Shankly's first full season at Anfield saw Liverpool again miss out by finishing third in the Second Division table — now it was Ipswich and Sheffield United who were galloping into the First Division while poor old Liverpool were the bridesmaids once more.

But Bill Shankly's team was taking shape. He brought Gordon Milne to Anfield for £12,000 and Milne proved to be one of his astute early signings. He was the son of Shankly's old Preston teammate, Jimmy Milne. Gerry Byrne took over from Ronnie Moran at left-back and Shankly went to South Yorkshire to sign Sheffield United's winger Kevin Lewis. Billy Liddell played just one more game for Liverpool before retiring in September with a record 492 appearances and the fantastic striking rate of 216 goals. In addition he had won twenty-eight caps for Scotland, scoring six goals, and had twice been selected for Great Britain teams. Small wonder that at his benefit match there were 38,000 fans who wished to pay homage to their hero.

But Liverpool's fans were not turning up in quite such numbers for the club's league matches and the season's average gate failed to top the 30,000 mark. Perhaps they were tired of supporting the 'nearly' side of the time. They should not have lost faith because Shankly was still busy rebuilding his side.

Liverpool won half their matches in 1960-1 and it was again the home points which the Reds dropped which separated them from the top at the end of the day. Nine points were lost at Anfield, including defeats at the hands of Southampton and Middlesbrough, and Shankly's team also failed to pick up any points on nine away grounds, although the margins of the defeats were no where near as alarming as had the reverses of previous seasons. The attack managed eighty-seven goals and Roger Hunt picked up fifteen in thirty-two matches in only his second season in league football, bringing his total in that time to thirty-six, which was a striking rate of which Billy Liddell would have been proud.

The FA Cup again proved to be a lean hunting ground for Liverpool and after beating Coventry City 3-1 at home — only a fair result because Coventry were then a mid-table Third Division side

Roger Hunt watches Liverpool's second half equaliser beat the despairing 'Boro goalkeeper at Ayrsome Park in August 1960.

Dave Hickson goes near with a header against Derby County at Anfield in October 1960.

with none of their later trappings (Jimmy Hill was to come much later) — they were beaten 2-0 by Sunderland in the fourth round. The Roker Park club had been one of the early contenders for the Second Division title and Liverpool did not beat them at all that season, losing the FA Cup match at Anfield and drawing both league encounters between the two sides.

In the end, third place was about right for Liverpool. They were not quite ready to return to the First Division yet. The top of the table read:

	P	W	D	L	F	A	Pts
1 Ipswich	42	26	7	9	100	55	59
2 Sheff Utd	42	26	6	10	81	51	58
3 Liverpool	42	21	10	11	87	58	52
4 Norwich	42	20	9	13	70	53	49
5 Middlesbrough	42	18	12	12	83	74	48
6 Sunderland	42	17	13	12	75	60	47
7 Swansea Town	42	18	11	13	77	73	47

But the end was in sight for the long-suffering Liverpool supporters. They would have to wait just one more season before the Reds took their rightful place in the top drawer of English soccer.

Second Division results 1960-1

	H	A
Brighton	2-0	1-3
Bristol Rovers	3-0	3-4
Charlton	2-1	3-1
Derby	1-0	4-1
Huddersfield	3-1	4-2
Ipswich	1-1	0-1
Leeds	2-0	2-2
Leyton Orient	5-0	3-1
Lincoln	2-0	2-1
Luton	2-2	1-2
Middlesbrough	3-4	1-1
Norwich	2-1	1-2
Plymouth	1-1	4-0
Portsmouth	3-3	2-2
Rotherham	2-1	0-1
Scunthorpe	3-2	3-2
Sheffield Utd	4-2	1-1
Southampton	0-1	1-4
Stoke	3-0	1-3
Sunderland	1-1	1-1
Swansea	4-0	0-2

Final League record

P	W	D	L	F	A	Pts	Pos
42	21	10	11	87	58	52	3rd

FA Cup

Rnd 3	Coventry	(h)	3-2
Rnd 4	Sunderland	(h)	0-2

Football League Cup

Rnd 2	Luton	(h)	1-1
Replay	Luton	(a)	5-2
Rnd 3	Southampton	(h)	1-2

1961-2

Complete with his latest signings, Bill Shankly carried Liverpool back into the First Division at last! This time there was to be no holding the Reds as they stormed away with the title, finishing eight points clear of Leyton Orient. Liverpool also just failed to score a century of league goals and they conceded only forty-three.

Ian St John signed for Liverpool from Motherwell for £37,000 when Shankly beat Newcastle United in the race for the Scotsman's signature; and big Ron Yeats became a Liverpool player when the Anfield club paid Dundee United £30,000. Shankly did well to get Liverpool to part with the money, for they had little cash to spend; but the directors had seen the sort of effect that Shankly had on players and they were never to regret a penny of the money that they gave him to spend on their behalf.

Liverpool clinch promotion with a 2-0 win over Southampton on April 21 1962. Ronnie Moran with Jimmy Melia on his right and Alan A'Court on his left, acknowledge the crowd.

Just as Liverpool had failed before because of poor starts to the season, so in 1961-2 they had the best possible start and it carried them right through. In the first eleven matches Liverpool dropped just one point and scored thirty-one goals with just four against. Roger Hunt ran riot with forty-one goals — a figure which broke the previous club individual record of Gordon Hodgson, and a figure which still stands today. Hunt also won the first of his thirty-four England caps when he played against Austria. Alan A'Court, Gerry Byrne, Jimmy Melia and Gordon Milne played in all Liverpool's matches and Yeats, Hunt, St John and Leishman were absent for just two each. Ian Callaghan came into the side and held his place for the rest of the season and in goal, Bert Slater gave way to Burnley's Jim Furnell.

Only seven games were lost as Liverpool stormed to the title, although one of them against Derby County at the Baseball Ground did football little credit. Derby won 2-0 and their victory — quite an epic for their own long-suffering fans — was marred by several incidents. One resulted in Derby's

Liverpool, Second Division Champions 1961-2. Back row left to right: Milne, Yeats, Furnell, Moran, Byrne, Leishman. Front row: Callaghan, Hunt, St John, Melia, A'Court.

Second Division results 1961-2

	H	A
Brighton	3-1	0-0
Bristol Rovers	2-0	2-0
Bury	5-0	3-0
Charlton	2-1	4-0
Derby	4-1	0-2
Huddersfield	1-1	2-1
Leeds	5-0	0-1
Leyton Orient	3-3	2-2
Luton	1-1	0-1
Middlesbrough	5-1	0-2
Newcastle	2-0	2-1
Norwich	5-4	2-1
Plymouth	2-1	3-2
Preston	4-1	3-1
Rotherham	4-1	0-1
Scunthorpe	2-1	1-1
Southampton	2-0	0-2
Stoke	2-1	0-0
Sunderland	3-0	4-1
Swansea	5-0	2-4
Walsall	6-1	1-1

Final League record

P	W	D	L	F	A	Pts	Pos
42	27	8	7	99	43	62	1st

FA Cup

Rnd 3	Chelsea	(h)	4-3
Rnd 4	Oldham	(a)	2-1
Rnd 5	Preston	(h)	0-0
Replay	Preston	(h)	0-0
Replay	Preston	(n)	0-1

centre-forward Bill Curry being felled on the halfway line while Liverpool were taking a corner over fifty yards away. Curry was later bundled over the railings which surround Derby's tight ground and a few hot-headed supporters ran on to the pitch before they were ushered off by the Derby players. Bill Shankly said he could not see anything wrong with either incident and Derby's manager Harry Storer agreed with him. Nevertheless, the Monday morning papers were full of the sort of headlines which have become depressingly familiar over the last twenty years.

The title was won by Shankly at the Melwood training ground where he plotted the downfall of opponents and toughened up his Liverpool troops until they could last the most gruelling afternoon's football. Leeds were crushed 5-0 and Walsall 6-1 at Anfield and Liverpool fell just one goal short of three figures.

In the FA Cup Liverpool beat First Division Chelsea (although Chelsea were to finish bottom of the table and exchange places with Liverpool it was still a good result), before being taken to three games by Preston before the Lancashire club won the second replay 1-0 and knocked out their county rivals. But it was the league which really mattered — and Liverpool were back! Here's how they finished:

	P	W	D	L	F	A	Pts
1 Liverpool	42	27	8	7	99	43	62
2 Leyton Orient	42	22	10	10	69	40	54
3 Sunderland	42	22	9	11	85	50	53
4 Scunthorpe	42	21	7	14	86	71	49

1962-3

If Liverpool supporters harboured any thoughts that their team would repeat history and storm straight to the top of the First Division, they were quickly dispelled in the first three matches of the season when Liverpool took just one point — and that a scrambled 2-2 draw at Maine Road. This season also brought the big freeze which was the worst interruption to Football League fixtures since Liverpool had won the title in that dreadful winter of 1946-7. Fixtures piled up again but Liverpool recovered from both their bad start and the effects of the disruption to climb into the top six in the table and also reach the semi-final of the FA Cup.

In the tenth match of the season Liverpool faced Everton in the first Merseyside league 'derby' for eleven seasons and over 70,000 fans saw a well-contested 2-2 draw. Later in the season the result of the Anfield return was also even when neither side could score. After losing 3-0 at Leicester, Shankly made another change, this time introducing another player whose name would ring from the Kop in the years to come. Tommy Lawrence replaced Jim Furnell in goal. Lawrence had spent years languishing in Liverpool's Central League side and he grabbed the opportunity of first team football with both hands.

Jim Furnell lost his place to Tommy Lawrence after the 3-0 defeat at Leicester on 13 October 1962.

Lawrence was joined by a fellow Scot, Willie Stevenson who was also spending most of his time in a reserve team, this time Rangers reserves. Shankly paid £27,000 for Stevenson and he soon made the midfield berth his own with Leishman being the man to drop out. In November, Liverpool earned a 3-3 draw at Old Trafford and from that moment their fortunes began to improve, although Leicester won 2-0 at Anfield, thanks mainly to Gordon Banks. Years later, another goalkeeper who had understudied Banks would prove just as capable of winning matches for Leicester almost single-handed.

When Tottenham Hotspur came to Liverpool over the Easter programme, the Reds had climbed

First Division results 1962-3

	H	A
Arsenal	2-1	2-2
Aston Villa	4-0	0-2
Birmingham	5-1	2-0
Blackburn	3-1	0-1
Blackpool	1-2	2-1
Bolton	1-0	0-1
Burnley	1-2	3-1
Everton	0-0	2-2
Fulham	2-1	0-0
Ipswich	1-1	2-2
Leicester	0-2	0-3
Leyton Orient	5-0	1-2
Man City	4-1	2-2
Man United	1-0	3-3
Nottm Forest	0-2	1-3
Sheffield Utd	2-0	0-0
Sheffield Wed	0-2	2-0
Tottenham	5-2	2-7
West Brom	2-2	0-1
West Ham	2-1	0-1
Wolves	4-1	2-3

Final League record

P	W	D	L	F	A	Pts	Pos
42	17	10	15	71	59	44	8th

FA Cup

Rnd 3	Wrexham	(a)	3-0
Rnd 4	Burnley	(a)	1-1
Replay	Burnley	(h)	2-1
Rnd 5	Arsenal	(a)	2-1
Rnd 6	West Ham	(h)	1-0
SF	Leicester	(n)	0-1

to sixth place and had good reason to be shocked when Spurs took a 2-0 lead. Then Stevenson pulled back a goal and Melia scored twice, and St John and Lewis once each as Liverpool staged a fightback to win 5-2; sadly, Spurs got their revenge and more besides when they hammered Liverpool 7-2 at White Lane, three days later. Jimmy Greaves scored four of the Tottenham goals. Liverpool's late challenge for the First Division title was aborted and they finished eighth.

In the FA Cup, Liverpool reached the semi-finals only after some hard struggles, including a replay with Burnley. They met Leicester City at Hillsborough in a bid to, not only reach the Wembley arena, but also to avenge two defeats by City in the league that season. It was not to be, and Leicester completed a hat-trick of wins over Liverpool when Mike Stringfellow scored the only goal of the game after twenty-five minutes.

There were no trophies to be seen in the Liverpool Boardroom as the season closed, but the Reds had re-established themselves as one of English soccer's leading forces. International honours had come flooding back to the club with five players being capped for England — A'Court, Byrne, Hunt, Melia and Milne — and Lawrence and St John winning Scottish caps. Lawrence won his first cap against the Republic of Ireland in Dublin just after the league season had finished, although he was to wait six years for his next appearance in the full Scotland team.

Jimmy Melia won his first England cap against Scotland at Wembley in April 1963.

1963-4

Before the start of the 1963-4 season Bill Shankly slipped over to Preston and gave them a cheque for £40,000 in return for the registration of Peter Thompson, Preston's left-winger. It was yet another example of Shankly's expertise in spotting a winner. Thompson became as important to Liverpool in the 'sixties as Billy Liddell had in the years after World War II. Liverpool also changed their strip from the familiar red shirts and white shorts which had served them for so long, and Shankly now dressed his men in all-red.

The season started in a manner unlikely to suggest that Liverpool would end the campaign as champions. Everton had taken the title the previous year and when Liverpool averaged only a point a game from their first nine games, and then went down 3-0 to Sheffield United, their immediate priority seemed to lie in the reverse end of the table. But, after losing at Bramall Lane, Liverpool beat Everton 2-1 at Anfield and then went on to take forty-seven points out of the next sixty, a run which culminated in a 5-0 defeat of Arsenal at Anfield in which Peter Thompson repaid most of his transfer fee with two bullet-like goals. Ironically, it was to Arsenal that the deposed Liverpool goalkeeper Jim Furnell had gone.

Three wins over Easter virtually clinched the championship and Liverpool finally finished ahead of Manchester United in a First Division which looked like this:

Liverpool v West Ham, September 1963. Peters gets the ball away from Hunt and out for a corner.

		P	W	D	L	F	A	Pts
1	Liverpool	42	26	5	11	92	45	57
2	Man United	42	23	7	12	90	62	53
3	Everton	42	21	10	11	84	64	52
4	Tottenham	42	22	7	13	97	81	51
5	Chelsea	42	20	10	12	72	56	50
6	Sheff Wed	42	19	11	12	84	67	49

In the FA Cup, Liverpool did rather less well. After thrashing Derby 5-0, they were forced to a replay by Port Vale (some 42,000 people saw the game at Burslem — a rare luxury for Vale), and then squeezed home 1-0 at Highbury before facing lowly Second Division side Swansea Town at Anfield. Swansea's goalkeeper Noel Dwyer played the game of his life that day. He saved a penalty from Ronnie Moran and helped Swansea to a shock 2-1 defeat of the team which would top the First Division that season. Swansea lost the semi-final 2-1 to Preston but that was small consolation to Liverpool. They had been mugged again.

But they were going on to win the title and Roger Hunt again weighed in with thirty-one goals from his forty-one appearances, helped by the emergence of Alf Arrowsmith which allowed St John to move back into the midfield. Jimmy Melia had gone to Wolverhampton Wanderers and another link with the old team was broken. As the season drew to a close Liverpool made plans for a tour to the United States where a Beatles-style reception awaited them. Then it was back home and earnest preparation for their first assault on Europe.

Manchester United's Harry Gregg smothers Arrowsmith's shot at Anfield in April 1964 – but Liverpool still won 3-0.

First Division results 1963-4

	H	A
Arsenal	5-0	1-1
Aston Villa	5-2	2-2
Birmingham	2-1	1-3
Blackburn	1-2	2-1
Blackpool	1-2	1-0
Bolton	2-0	2-1
Burnley	2-0	3-0
Chelsea	2-1	3-1
Everton	2-1	1-3
Fulham	2-0	0-1
Ipswich	6-0	2-1
Leicester	0-1	2-0
Man United	3-0	1-0
Nottm Forest	1-2	0-0
Sheffield Utd	6-1	0-3
Sheffield Wed	3-1	2-2
Stoke	6-1	1-3
Tottenham	3-1	3-1
West Brom	1-0	2-2
West Ham	1-2	0-1
Wolves	6-0	3-1

Final League record

P	W	D	L	F	A	Pts	Pos
42	26	5	11	92	45	57	1st

FA Cup

Rnd 3	Derby	(h)	5-0
Rnd 4	Port Vale	(h)	0-0
Replay	Port Vale	(a)	2-1
Rnd 5	Arsenal	(a)	1-0
Rnd 6	Swansea	(h)	1-2

1964-5

Although they slid down to seventh position in the First Division, Liverpool still have plenty to remember the 1964-5 season; besides their first taste of European Cup football, the Reds also went to Wembley and won the FA Cup for the first time in their history by beating Leeds United 2-1 after extra-time. And as if that was not enough, they also went right through to the European semi-finals for what could have been an historic 'double'.

Liverpool's European baptism was not one of fire. In the first round they played the Icelandic champions of Reykjavik and crushed them 11-1 on aggregate with two new faces both getting a share of the goals. Phil Chisnall had signed from Manchester United and Gordon Wallace won his place after some fine displays in Liverpool's Central League team. In the next round Liverpool beat Belgian champions Anderlecht 4-0 on aggregate and Tommy Smith made his first appearance on the European stage he was to grace in the coming seasons. When Liverpool could not settle their quarter-final leg with Cologne after three drawn games, the Reds went into the semi-final in the most unsatisfactory manner when they won the toss of a coloured disc — penalty deciders were a thing of the future.

That is where Liverpool's European luck ended. After beating Italian champions Inter Milan 3-1 at Anfield in the first-leg of the semi-final, the Reds were subjected to a tirade of abuse in Italy and they lost 3-0 after Inter had scored two highly controversial goals — one when the Italians appeared to score straight from an indirect free-kick, and the other when the ball was kicked out of Tommy Lawrence's hands.

Liverpool *did* win the FA Cup, although that was not without its fraught moments. A 2-1 win over West Bromwich Albion in their third round tussle at the Hawthorns was only achieved after Albion had missed a penalty; and Stockport County, the club in ninety-second place in the Football League, had managed a 1-1 draw at Anfield before Liverpool removed them 2-0 in the replay. Then Bolton were beaten 1-0 in the fifth round and that man Gordon Banks did all he could to stop Liverpool in the quarter-finals. At the end of 180 minutes football, Roger Hunt's goal at Anfield was the one which finally broke the deadlock. Chelsea, then managed by Tommy Docherty, were beaten easily in the semi-final, Liverpool triumphing 2-0 at Villa Park, and so to Wembley and Leeds United, the team which would finish second in the First Division that season.

Liverpool had problems. Gordon Milne's injury ruled him out of the final and Geoff Strong came into his place. And when Gerry Byrne broke his collar bone after only a few minutes, things looked decidedly black for Liverpool. Bravely, Byrne nursed the injury through the rest of the game without Leeds knowing how badly hurt he was, and after ninety minutes there was no score. In extra-time, Hunt made it 1-0 to Liverpool before Billy Bremner equalised. Then Ian St John hit home the winner and all Merseyside (with the possible exception of Goodison Park!) went wild. The Reds would lose out in Europe and they had already lost the First Division title. But the FA Cup had come to Anfield at long last.

Liverpool v Aston Villa, September 1964. Hunt's header finds the net but he is offside. The Reds went on to win 5-1, however.

First Division results 1964-5

	H	A
Arsenal	3-2	0-0
Aston Villa	5-1	1-0
Birmingham	4-3	0-0
Blackburn	3-2	2-3
Blackpool	2-2	3-2
Burnley	1-1	5-1
Chelsea	2-0	0-4
Everton	0-4	1-2
Fulham	3-2	1-1
Leeds	2-1	2-4
Leicester	0-1	0-2
Man United	0-2	0-3
Nottm Forest	2-0	2-2
Sheffield Utd	3-1	0-3
Sheffield Wed	4-2	0-1
Stoke	3-2	1-1
Sunderland	0-0	3-2
Tottenham	1-1	0-3
West Brom	0-3	0-3
West Ham	2-2	1-2
Wolves	2-1	3-1

Final League record

P	W	D	L	F	A	Pts	Pos
42	17	10	15	67	73	44	7th

FA Cup

Rnd 3	West Brom	(a)	2-1
Rnd 4	Stockport	(h)	1-1
Replay	Stockport	(a)	2-0
Rnd 5	Bolton	(a)	1-0
Rnd 6	Leicester	(a)	0-0
Replay	Leicester	(h)	1-0
SF	Chelsea	VP	2-0
	(VP = Villa Park)		
Final	Leeds	W	2-1
	(W = Wembley)		

(after extra time)

European Cup

Rnd 1	(1st leg)	Reykjavik	(a)	5-0
Rnd 1	(2nd leg)	Reykjavik	(h)	6-1
Rnd 2	(1st leg)	Anderlecht	(h)	3-0
Rnd 2	(2nd leg)	Anderlecht	(a)	1-0
Rnd 3	(1st leg)	Cologne	(a)	0-0
Rnd 3	(2nd leg)	Cologne	(h)	0-0
Replay	Cologne		R	2-2
	(R = Rotterdam)			

Liverpool won on toss of a coin

SF	(1st leg)	Inter Milan	(h)	3-1
SF	(2nd leg)	Inter Milan	(a)	0-3

Ian St John scores Liverpool's fourth goal against Sheffield Wednesday at Anfield in January 1965.

St John cracks home a Liverpool goal in the FA Cup Final against Leeds United at Wembley.

1965-6

Liverpool were champions again! The First Division trophy came once more to Anfield, although the FA Cup made a speedy departure when Liverpool were beaten 2-1 at home by Chelsea in the third round. Liverpool also reached the final of the European Cup-winners Cup, but here, too, they failed to stay the course and lost to the West German cup holders in Glasgow.

Liverpool were well on their way to recapturing the championship quite early on in the season. They went to the top of the First Division well before Christmas and clinched the title on 30 April when they gained revenge over Chelsea by beating them 2-1 at Anfield (the Reds had already won 1-0 at Stamford Bridge) to win the title for the seventh time. Liverpool had some big victories and Blackburn, West Ham, Everton and Northampton each had five goals put past them by a rampant Liverpool attack which finished up with seventy-nine goals, of which Roger Hunt scored thirty. Liverpool lost just seven games and only two of these were at home when Sheffield United and Leeds United had each sneaked 1-0 wins before skipping back over the Pennines. The final top placings were:

Gordon Milne heads Liverpool's third goal in the 4-1 over Blackpool on 19 February 1966.

	P	W	D	L	F	A	Pts
1 Liverpool	42	26	9	7	79	34	61
2 Leeds Utd	42	23	9	10	79	38	55
3 Burnley	42	24	7	11	79	47	55
4 Man United	42	18	15	9	84	59	51

Liverpool's quest for the Cup-winners Cup started in Turin where the Reds faced the famous Italian team Juventus, who had lifted the Italian FA Cup the previous season. After the first-leg, Liverpool trailed by a single goal. At Anfield, Lawler and Strong netted the goals which put Liverpool further along the road to the final, Lawler's goal being typical of the many 'sneak' efforts which the defender would snaffle for Liverpool.

In the very next round, against Belgian club Liege, Lawler scored two more and Thompson one as Liverpool opened up a 3-1 lead after their home first-leg; in Belgium, Hunt and St John saw Liverpool extend that lead. The quarter-final brought the famous Hungarians of Honved to Anfield after Liverpool had drawn 0-0 in Hungary. Lawler, again, and St John helped Liverpool to a 2-0 win at home and then came the semi-final tie everyone had been waiting for — Liverpool v Celtic. After losing the away leg 1-0, Liverpool soon pulled level and finished 2-1 up on aggregate through Smith and Strong. Celtic fans decided that the next best thing to beating Liverpool was cheering on some other team to do just that, and when Liverpool ran out at Hampden Park, the West Germans of Borussia Dortmund seemed to have almost as much support. The night was stormy and although Roger Hunt overcame an ankle injury to score, Dortmund went on to win through Held and a Ron Yeats own goal.

As England — with Byrne, Hunt and Callaghan in their squad — prepared to win the 1966 World Cup, Liverpool looked back on another championship year and then looked forward to the coming season when they would once again compete with the cream of Europe. Roger Hunt would have his own personal highlight before that, winning a World Cup winners medal with his country and obtaining his own revenge over the West Germans who had knocked his side out of the Cup-Winners Cup.

Cup-winners Cup

Rnd 1	(1st leg)	Juventus	(a)	0-1
Rnd 1	(2nd leg)	Juventus	(h)	2-0
Rnd 2	(1st leg)	Liege	(h)	3-1
Rnd 2	(2nd leg)	Liege	(a)	2-1
Rnd 3	(1st leg)	Honved	(a)	0-0
Rnd 3	(2nd leg)	Honved	(h)	2-0
SF	(1st leg)	Celtic	(a)	0-1
SF	(2nd leg)	Celtic	(h)	2-0
Final		Borussia Dortmund	G	1-2
		(G = Glasgow)		

First Division results 1965-6

	H	A
Arsenal	4-2	1-0
Aston Villa	3-1	3-0
Blackburn	5-2	4-1
Blackpool	4-1	3-2
Burnley	2-1	0-2
Chelsea	2-1	1-0
Everton	5-0	0-0
Fulham	2-1	0-2
Leeds	0-1	1-0
Leicester	1-0	3-1
Man United	2-1	0-2
Newcastle	2-0	0-0
Northampton	5-0	0-0
Nottm Forest	4-0	1-1
Sheffield Utd	0-1	0-0
Sheffield Wed	1-0	2-0
Stoke	2-0	0-0
Sunderland	4-0	2-2
Tottenham	1-0	1-2
West Brom	2-2	0-3
West Ham	1-1	5-1

Final League record

P	W	D	L	F	A	Pts	Pos
42	26	9	7	79	34	61	1st

FA Cup

| Rnd 3 | Chelsea | (h) | 1-2 |

Milne shows his jubilation after Hunt scores the winner against Chelsea in April 1966.

1966-7

Since returning to the First Division Liverpool had won the League Championship twice, the FA Cup once, and had reached both the final of the European Cup-winners Cup and the semi-final of the European Cup. And those honours had all been achieved within the space of four seasons. But in 1966-7 Liverpool brought no trophies to Merseyside although it is a measure of the immensely high standard which the club has set itself, that we perhaps consider it to be a season of failure.

Liverpool's main objective was the European Cup and in this competition they were knocked out by a team which would soon become one of the greatest forces in European soccer — the flying Dutchmen of Ajax Amsterdam. Liverpool's quest for the European Cup began in September when they were drawn against the Romanian champions, Petrolui Ploesti. The first-leg was played at Anfield on 28 September and Ian St John and Ian Callaghan gave Liverpool a 2-0 win which was to prove to be less than adequate to see them through. In those days, if games were tied after two legs, the teams had to go to a third match and so Roger Hunt's goal in the 3-1 defeat in Romania was not enough to keep Liverpool clear. At that time, away goals did not count double. Eventually, St John and Thompson made sure and Liverpool were through 2-0.

St John sees his shot blocked by the Aston Villa goalkeeper during the 1-0 win over the Midland club in February 1967.

When the second round draw pitted the Reds against Ajax, there was little apprehension in the Anfield camp. Dutch football was not a world power, even though their FA was the oldest in the world outside Britain, and little was known about them. But Ajax had some shocks in store and guided by the brilliant — and, at the time, largely unheard of — Johan Cruyff, the Dutchmen powered their way to a 5-1 win over Liverpool with Chris Lawler snatching a consolation goal for the Reds. At Anfield one week later, Liverpool could only draw 2-2 and the Reds were out 7-3 on aggregate. It was a crushing experience but one from which Shankly's Liverpool would learn much.

In the FA Cup Liverpool allowed Watford to force a goalless draw at Vicarage Road before the Reds won the Anfield replay and in the fourth round against Aston Villa, Liverpool hearts were in their mouths until the Reds scraped through 1-0; a fifth round tie at Goodison Park saw Liverpool's cup run come to an end when Everton won 1-0. A defeat by Everton is always hard to swallow and when it comes in the cup it is doubly difficult to take.

As for the First Division, Liverpool went down to fifth place. West Bromwich Albion and Blackpool won at Anfield and it was from Bloomfield Road that Shankly brought another young player who would lead Liverpool into the Seventies. Emlyn Hughes joined Liverpool from Blackpool for a Liverpool record fee of £65,000. It was to be money

Liverpool 1966-7. Back row left to right: Strong, Smith, Yeats, Lawrence, Lawler, Stevenson, McDougall. Front row: Callaghan, Hunt, St John, Graham, Thompson.

well spent. Shankly knew that he must make more changes in a team which was in decline and the fact was underlined when relegated Blackpool won 3-1 at Anfield on the last day of the season. The gate of some 28,000 also gave rise to concern. Gordon Milne was transferred to Blackpool and Stevenson went to Stoke City's Victoria Ground. Both players had given their all for Liverpool but, sadly, neither of them now fitted into Shankly's future plans.

FA Cup

Rnd 3	Watford	(a)	0-0
Replay	Watford	(h)	3-1
Rnd 4	Aston Villa	(h)	1-0
Rnd 5	Everton	(a)	0-1

European Cup

1st Rnd (1st leg)	Petrolui	(h)	2-0
1st Rnd (2nd leg)	Petrolui	(a)	1-3
Replay	Petrolui	(B)	2-0
(B = Brussels)			
2nd Rnd (1st leg)	Ajax	(a)	1-5
2nd Rnd (2nd leg)	Ajax	(h)	2-2

First Division results 1966-7

	H	A
Arsenal	0-0	1-1
Aston Villa	1-0	3-2
Blackpool	1-3	2-1
Burnley	2-0	0-1
Chelsea	2-1	2-1
Everton	0-0	1-3
Fulham	2-2	2-2
Leeds	5-0	1-2
Leicester	3-2	1-2
Man City	3-2	1-2
Man United	0-0	2-2
Newcastle	3-1	2-0
Nottm Forest	4-0	1-1
Sheffield Utd	1-0	1-0
Sheffield Wed	1-1	1-0
Southampton	2-1	2-1
Stoke	2-1	0-2
Sunderland	2-2	2-2
Tottenham	0-0	1-2
West Brom	0-1	1-2
West Ham	2-0	1-1

Final League record

P	W	D	L	F	A	Pts	Pos
42	19	13	10	64	47	51	5th

1967-8

In the close season of 1967 Shankly made two important signings for Liverpool. Big centre-forward Tony Hateley ('he's had more clubs than Arnold Palmer' was the joke) arrived at his latest after Liverpool had paid Chelsea £96,000; and Shankly laid out another £18,000 for Scunthorpe United's goalkeeper Ray Clemence. It was chicken feed when one remembers that Clemence has become England's number one goalkeeper, keeping the brilliant Peter Shilton out of the international side.

Liverpool's final position of fifth in 1966-7 meant that they qualified for European competition again, this time in the Fairs Cup. The Reds won through to the third round before Hungarian side Ferencvaros won both at Anfield and behind the Iron Curtain; and after finishing third in the First Division, being knocked out of the FA Cup in the sixth round, and losing in the Football League Cup's second round, Liverpool again had a bare season.

Tony Hateley was soon on the mark for his new club, scoring both goals in Liverpool's 2-0 win over Malmo FF in the first round first-leg of the Fairs Cup in Sweden; Yeats and Hunt made the aggregate a comfortable 4-1 in Liverpool and that gave the Reds a second round tie with West Germany's Munich 1860.

The first-leg was at Anfield and Liverpool went wild, winning 8-0. Their goalscorers that night were Hunt (2), Callaghan (2), St John, Hateley, Thompson, and Smith from the penalty spot. Liverpool were already through to the third round and their 2-1 win in Munich was academic. There was to be no happy New Year for Liverpool, however. Ferencvaros won both legs of their third round tie with the Reds 1-0 and Anfield turned its thoughts to the FA Cup. Bolton Wanderers had already knocked Liverpool out of the Football League Cup after a replay in what was the Reds first League Cup match since the 1960-1 season.

The third round of the FA Cup presented Liverpool with a difficult tie at Bournemouth and they were happy to come home with a 0-0 draw before completing the job at Anfield; Walsall, too, managed a goalless draw at Fellows Park before going down heavily at Anfield and in the fifth round, Liverpool faced yet another replay against Tottenham Hotspur before they reached the quarter-finals. Their match at The Hawthorns was a goalless draw and when West Brom drew 1-1 at Anfield, the tie had to go to a third game before WBA took it 2-1; in reaching that stage of the competition Liverpool had played nine games — more than the

Roger Hunt heads the ball home but is given offside during the game with Leicester at Filbert Street in October 1967.

eventual FA Cup winners Everton. Battle weary Liverpool were never going to win the First Division after that and the top two places went to Manchester with City coming out on top.

Liverpool were just short of achieving the sort of record which would have won the championship as the top of the table shows:

	P	W	D	L	F	A	Pts
1 Man City	42	26	6	10	86	43	58
2 Man United	42	24	8	10	89	55	56
3 Liverpool	42	22	11	9	71	40	55
4 Leeds	42	22	9	11	71	41	53
5 Everton	42	23	6	13	67	40	52
6 Chelsea	42	18	12	12	62	68	48

Peter Thompson and Roger Hunt challenge Leeds goalkeeper Harvey at Elland Road in May 1968.

Football League Cup

| Rnd 2 | Bolton | (h) | 1-1 |
| Replay | Bolton | (a) | 2-3 |

Fairs Cup

Rnd 1	(1st leg)	Malmo	(a)	2-0
Rnd 1	(2nd leg)	Malmo	(h)	2-1
Rnd 2	(1st leg)	Munich	(h)	8-0
Rnd 2	(2nd leg)	Munich	(a)	1-2
Rnd 3	(1st leg)	Ferencvaros	(a)	0-1
Rnd 3	(2nd leg)	Ferencvaros	(h)	0-1

First Division results 1967-8

	H	A
Arsenal	2-0	0-2
Burnley	3-2	1-1
Chelsea	3-1	1-3
Coventry	1-0	1-1
Everton	1-0	0-1
Fulham	4-1	1-1
Leeds	2-0	2-1
Leicester	3-1	1-2
Man City	1-1	0-0
Man United	1-2	2-1
Newcastle	6-0	1-1
Nottm Forest	6-1	1-0
Sheffield Utd	1-2	1-1
Sheffield Wed	1-0	2-1
Southampton	2-0	0-1
Stoke	2-1	1-2
Sunderland	2-1	1-1
Tottenham	1-1	1-1
West Brom	4-1	2-0
West Ham	3-1	0-1
Wolves	2-1	1-1

Final League record

P	W	D	L	F	A	Pts	Pos
42	22	11	9	71	40	55	3rd

FA Cup

Rnd 3	Bournemouth	(a)	0-0
Replay	Bournemouth	(h)	4-1
Rnd 4	Walsall	(a)	0-0
Replay	Walsall	(h)	5-2
Rnd 5	Tottenham	(a)	1-1
Replay	Tottenham	(h)	2-1
Rnd 6	West Brom	(a)	0-0
Replay	West Brom	(h)	1-1
Replay	West Brom	(n)	1-2

1968-9

Bill Shankly was never a man to be afraid of putting money where his judgement lay and at the start of 1968-9 the Liverpool manager paid Wolverhampton Wanderers £100,000 for eighteen-year-old Alun Evans, a striker. It was an astonishing amount of money to lay out for a young player at that time but Shankly clearly felt that Evans's potential more than justified the sum. When Evans scored two goals in Liverpool's first two matches, it seemed that his faith was already repaid.

But it was another disappointing season and again, Liverpool failed to win anything. They were back in the Fairs Cup but their run came to an abrupt and most unsatisfactory end against the northern Spanish club Bilbao. Liverpool had lost the first-leg in Spain by 2-1, but Hunt's goal gave them hope for the return leg. Liverpool won that all right, but only by the same score and with the aggregate now level, there was one of those ludicrous situations where the sides tossed a coloured disc. Liverpool had been lucky against Cologne — they were unlucky against Bilbao and Liverpool's European challenge lay in ruins as the plastic disc fell into the Anfield mud and signalled the thumbs-down for the Reds.

The Football League Cup held no greater rewards and after beating Sheffield United, and laying the ghost of Swansea, Liverpool fell at Highbury in the fourth round; in the FA Cup, the old 'bogey' side of Leicester City drew at Filbert Street and then sent Liverpool out 1-0 at Anfield. It was a sorry season for Liverpool, so far as knockout cups went.

In the league Liverpool eventually finished runners-up, although their final position sounds better than it was when one considers that the Reds were a clear six points behind champions Leeds United. Merseyside, as a whole, could be pleased that Everton came up into third place to give a northern dominance to the First Division table. The underlying factor behind the season's league statistics was that Liverpool had by far the best defensive record of the ninety-two clubs which make up the Football League. Only twenty-four goals found their way into the Liverpool net, and even allowing for the fact that fewer and fewer goals were being scored in any sort of football, thanks to the new tactics which were emerging from Europe, it was a fine performance and one which heralded the start of a Liverpool tradition of being 'mean at the back'. Only two sides — Nottingham Forest and Tottenham Hotspur — managed to score twice against Liverpool in 1968-9 and the Reds kept a clean sheet on no fewer than twenty-one occasions. Their biggest win was a superb 6-0 defeat of Wolves at Molineux.

Callaghan scores the third Liverpool goal past Jim Montgomery of Sunderland at Anfield in August 1968.

Liverpool's record was impressive and only the fact that they had to contend with such a superbly efficient Leeds United team cost them the title. Liverpool's final tally of sixty-one points would have been good enough to finish top in the previous two seasons. Here are the final placings at the top of the 1968-9 First Division:

	P	W	D	L	F	A	Pts
1 Leeds Utd	42	27	13	2	66	26	67
2 Liverpool	42	25	11	6	63	24	61
3 Everton	42	21	15	6	77	36	57
4 Arsenal	42	22	12	8	56	27	56
5 Chelsea	42	20	10	12	73	53	50
6 Tottenham	42	14	17	11	61	51	45

FA Cup

Rnd 3	Doncaster	(h)	2-0
Rnd 4	Burnley	(h)	2-1
Rnd 5	Leicester	(a)	0-0
Replay	Leicester	(h)	0-1

Football League Cup

Rnd 2	Sheffield Utd	(h)	4-0
Rnd 3	Swansea	(h)	2-0
Rnd 4	Arsenal	(a)	1-2

Fairs Cup

Rnd 1	(1st leg)	Bilbao	(a)	1-2
Rnd 2	(2nd leg)	Bilbao	(h)	2-1

Liverpool lost on toss of a coin

First Division results 1968-9

	H	A
Arsenal	1-1	1-1
Burnley	1-1	4-0
Chelsea	2-1	2-1
Coventry	2-0	0-0
Everton	1-1	0-0
Ipswich	4-0	2-0
Leeds	0-0	0-1
Leicester	4-0	2-1
Man City	2-1	0-1
Man United	2-0	0-1
Newcastle	2-1	1-1
Nottm Forest	0-2	1-0
QPR	2-0	2-1
Sheffield Wed	1-0	2-1
Southampton	1-0	0-2
Stoke	2-1	0-0
Sunderland	4-1	2-0
Tottenham	1-0	1-2
West Brom	1-0	0-0
West Ham	2-0	1-1
Wolves	1-0	6-0

Final League record

P	W	D	L	F	A	Pts	Pos
42	25	11	6	63	24	61	2nd

Chris Lawler goes up with Chelsea's Peter Bonetti at Anfield in November 1968. Liverpool won 2-1.

1969-70

In 1969 two more players joined the Liverpool fold and although they went into the reserves, both Alec Lindsay and Larry Lloyd would soon force their way through into the Reds first team. Lloyd came from Bristol Rovers as a big, strapping centre-half; Lindsay was Bury's full-back before he came to Anfield. The combined signing fee was not much more than £100,000 — another Shankly bargain.

Yet Shankly's rebuilding programme was not complete and in 1969-70 Liverpool again failed to register any success in the form of silverware. They were again involved in the Fairs Cup and could not have enjoyed an easier start to the competition than their first round draw against Irish part-timers Dundalk. At Anfield on 16 September 1969, poor Dundalk were crushed 10-0 by the Liverpool machine. The goals were evenly shared with two each going to Evans, Smith and Graham, and one each to Lawler, Lindsay, Thompson and Callaghan. In Ireland the Reds increased that aggregate to a massive 14-0 through Thompson (2), Lawler and Callaghan. That brought Liverpool into direct confrontation with the Portuguese club Setubal. Setubal won 1-0 in Portugal and then scored two vital away goals in going down at Liverpool on the night, but through to the next round on the new away goals rule. Smith scored from the penalty spot, and Evans and Hunt helped Liverpool to a 3-2 scoreline, only to see them miss out.

Liverpool's unhappy association with the Football League Cup continued when Manchester City knocked them out of the third round after the Reds had won at Watford. In the FA Cup it was Watford who sprang the surprise of the day on Liverpool when the Reds went to Vicarage Road for a sixth round game which should have seen them nicely into the semi-finals. Coventry (after a replay), Wrexham and Leicester (after a replay) had been dismissed from the cup and even allowing for the fact that Peter Thompson and Tommy Smith did not play, Watford's feat in winning 1-0 cannot be underestimated, although Liverpool seemed to have little appetite for a game which should have sent them to within ninety minutes of Wembley.

Knocked out of all three cups, Liverpool had the First Division championship to fight for, but they could only finish fifth. The defence conceded forty-two goals after its golden year of 1968-9 and when the forwards could manage only two more goals than the previous season's total, it was fairly obvious that Liverpool would finish lower down the table. Eleven games were lost, including home defeats by Manchester United, Arsenal and Derby,

Liverpool v Chelsea, August 1969. Strong lifts Yeats off the ground as Graham runs in to say 'Great goal!'

who were playing their first First Division game at Anfield since 1952-3 season. Liverpool were also beaten 4-0 at the Baseball Ground by Brian Clough's rampant Rams.

One face was missing from the Anfield scene. Roger Hunt had played his last game for Liverpool and in 1969-70 he was scoring goals for Lancashire neighbours Bolton Wanderers. Yeats, St John and Lawrence also found themselves out of the Liverpool first team as Bill Shankly prepared to face the new decade with a new-look Liverpool. Although Anfield fans could bemoan the club's lack of success over the past few seasons, Shankly had won titles and cups for them — and he would do it again before leaving the machinery to go on relentlessly into the 'eighties. Liverpool were about to become the team of the decade.

Liverpool 1969-70. Emlyn Hughes is taken off guard as he shares a joke with Ian St John.

First Division results 1969-70

	H	A
Arsenal	0-1	1-2
Burnley	3-3	5-1
Chelsea	4-1	1-2
Coventry	2-1	3-2
Crystal Palace	3-0	3-1
Derby	0-2	0-4
Everton	0-2	3-0
Ipswich	2-0	2-2
Leeds	0-0	1-1
Man City	3-2	2-0
Man United	1-4	0-1
Newcastle	0-0	0-1
Nottm Forest	1-1	0-1
Sheffield Wed	3-0	1-1
Southampton	4-1	1-0
Stoke	3-1	2-0
Sunderland	2-0	1-0
Tottenham	0-0	2-0
West Brom	1-1	2-2
West Ham	2-0	0-1
Wolves	0-0	1-0

Final League record

P	W	D	L	F	A	Pts	Pos
42	20	11	11	65	42	51	5th

FA Cup

Rnd 3	Coventry	(a)	1-1
Replay	Coventry	(h)	3-0
Rnd 4	Wrexham	(h)	3-1
Rnd 5	Leicester	(h)	0-0
Replay	Leicester	(a)	2-0
Rnd 6	Watford	(a)	0-1

Football League Cup

Rnd 2	Watford	(a)	2-1
Rnd 3	Man City	(a)	2-3

Fairs Cup

Rnd 1	(1st leg)	Dundalk	(h)	10-0
Rnd 1	(2nd leg)	Dundalk	(a)	4-0
Rnd 2	(1st leg)	Setubal	(a)	0-1
Rnd 2	(2nd leg)	Setubal	(h)	3-2

Liverpool lost on away goals rule

1970-1

Liverpool Football Club's march into the 'seventies — a decade which they were to dominate — began with an FA Cup Final appearance and a place in the semi-finals of the Fairs Cup, as well as reaching fifth place in the First Division again. It was a record good enough to satisfy dozens and dozens of lesser clubs — but for the Super Reds of Anfield it was only the beginning.

One of Liverpool's most memorable games of the season came on 21 November when they met Everton at Anfield in the 103rd Merseyside 'derby' match. Yet the first forty-five minutes promised nothing of the epic second half which was to follow. Too often, games between Liverpool and Everton had failed to live up to the occasion and the first half of this match was unmemorable — good football was overawed by tension and the period was littered with petty fouls.

Two weeks previously, John Toshack had joined the Reds for a club record fee of £110,000 paid to Cardiff City, while faces like Roger Hunt, Ron Yeats, Ian St John and Tommy Lawrence were all missing. Hunt had gone to Bolton; the rest were in Liverpool's reserves. After nineteen minutes of the second half against Everton, Liverpool suddenly found themselves trailing 2-0. First, Alan Whittle capitalised on a mistake by Tommy Smith; then Joe Royle headed home John Morrissey's centre and it appeared that Liverpool were in for a humiliating defeat. But five minutes later, Smith found Heighway and the Eire international — with his First Division career only one month old — scored a brilliant goal by beating the Everton defence single-handed and then delivering a superb shot past Andy Rankin. Seven minutes after that Liverpool drew level. Again Heighway devastated the Everton defence before centering for Toshack to leap high to head home. Another eight minutes went by and Liverpool were in front. It was full-back Chris Lawler who finished off Everton. Lindsay curled over a centre, Toshack flicked it on with his head, and there was Lawler to crack the ball past Rankin. Liverpool won 3-2 and Shankly's new young lions had proved they had all the character in the world with this epic fight-back.

They reached the FA Cup Final by beating Aldershot in the third round and then wiping out the memory of that humiliation by Swansea with a 3-0 win over the Welshmen at Anfield; then Southampton and Spurs (after a replay) brought Liverpool to the semi-final and face-to-face with — Everton! At Manchester United's Old Trafford stadium, Liverpool beat their old rivals for the second time that season, again thanks to their young starlets. The winning goal came from Brian Hall — like Heighway, not long out of university. But 1970-1 was to be the year that Arsenal won the 'double' and in the FA Cup Final at Wembley they took the second leg of this historic achievement by beating the Reds 2-1 after extra-time, through Kelly and George.

Liverpool's interest in the League Cup was ended by Swindon after the Reds had struggled to beat lowly Mansfield Town, but they retained an interest in the Fairs Cup until the last four. Liverpool beat some well-known names on the way to the semi-finals with Bayern Munich falling 3-0 at Anfield. Bayern, who were soon to win the European Cup three times in a row, were stunned by an Evans hat-trick. But England's place in the Fairs Cup Final was to go, not to Liverpool, but to Leeds. Billy Bremner scored the only goal of the 180 minutes football of the two legs and it was the Yorkshire club which went on to win the trophy against Juventus of Italy.

There was one other highlight of that season. In April 1971, Shankly went to Scunthorpe to pay £35,000 for a young player — his name was Kevin Keegan.

Action in the Liverpool goalmouth during the 1971 FA Cup Final against Arsenal.

Heighway scores for Liverpool as the 1971 FA Cup goes into extra-time.

First Division results 1970-1

Aug 15   Burnley.............. (a)   2-1
(Hughes, Evans; 26,702)

Aug 17   Blackpool............ (a)   0-0
(27,000)

Aug 22   Huddersfield......... (h)   4-0
(Evans 2, McLaughlin 2; 52,628)

Aug 25   Crystal Palace....... (h)   1-1
(Graham: 47,612)

Aug 29   West Brom............ (a)   1-1
(Evans; 31,624)

Sep 5   Man United........... (h)   1-1
(Evans; 52,541)

Sep 12   Newcastle............ (a)   0-0
(35,501)

Sep 19   Nottm Forest......... (h)   3-0
Evans, Graham, Thompson; 40,676)

Sep 26   Southampton.......... (a)   0-1
(26,155)

Oct 3   Chelsea.............. (h)   1-0
(Evans; 46,196)

Oct 10   Tottenham............ (a)   0-1
(44,457)

Oct 17   Burnley.............. (h)   2-0
(Heighway, Yeats; 40,804)

Oct 24   Ipswich.............. (a)   0-1
(22,577)

Oct 31   Wolves............... (h)   2-0
(Evans, Smith pen; 45,391)

Nov 7   Derby................ (a)   0-0
(33,004)

Nov 14   Coventry............. (h)   0-0
(50,303)

Nov 21   Everton.............. (h)   3-2
(Heighway, Toshack, Lawler; 53,777)

Nov 28   Arsenal.............. (a)   0-2
(45,097)

Dec 5   Leeds................ (h)   1-1
(Toshack; 51,357)

Dec 12   West Ham............. (a)   2-1
(Whitham, Boersma; 27,459)

Dec 19   Huddersfield......... (h)   0-0
(25,033)

Dec 26   Stoke................ (h)   0-0
(47,103)

Jan 9   Blackpool............ (h)   2-2
(Heighway, opp own goal; 42,939)

Jan 12   Man City............. (h)   0-0
(45,985)

65

Jan 16	Crystal Palace	(a)	0-1
(28,253)			
Jan 30	Arsenal	(h)	2-0
(Smith pen, Toshack; 43,847)			
Feb 6	Leeds	(a)	1-0
(Toshack; 48,425)			
Feb 16	West Ham	(h)	1-0
(Toshack; 38,032)			
Feb 20	Everton	(a)	0-0
(57,000)			
Feb 27	Wolves	(a)	0-1
(32,290)			
Mar 13	Coventry	(a)	0-1
(27,687)			
Mar 20	Derby	(h)	2-0
(Opp own goal, Lawler; 40,990)			
Mar 29	Ipswich	(h)	2-1
(Evans, Graham; 41,817)			
Apr 2	West Brom	(h)	1-1
(Evans; 43,580)			
Apr 6	Newcastle	(h)	1-1
(Lawler; 44,289)			
Apr 10	Stoke	(a)	1-0
(Thompson; 28,810)			
Apr 12	Chelsea	(a)	0-1
(38,705)			
Apr 17	Tottenham	(h)	0-0
(49,363)			
Apr 19	Man United	(a)	2-0
(Heighway, opp own goal; 44,004)			
Apr 24	Nottm Forest	(a)	1-0
(Hall; 20,678)			
Apr 26	Man City	(a)	2-2
(Graham 2; 17,975)			
May 1	Southampton	(h)	1-0
(Hughes; 38,427)			

Final League record

P	W	D	L	F	A	Pts	Pos
42	17	17	8	42	24	51	5th

League goalscorers: Evans 10, Graham 5, Toshack 5, Heighway 4, Lawler 3, own goals 3, Hughes 2, McLaughlin 2, Thompson 2, Smith 2, Yeats, Boersma, Whitham, Hall.

Football League Cup

Sep 8	(Rd 2) Mansfield	(a)	0-0
(12,532)			
Sep 22	(replay) Mansfield	(h)	3-2
(Hughes, Smith, Evans; 31,087)			
Oct 6	(Rd 3) Swindon	(a)	0-2
(23,992)			

Football League Cup goalscorers: Evans, Hughes, Smith

FA Cup

Jan 2	(Rd 3) Aldershot	(h)	1-0
(McLaughlin; 45,500)			
Jan 23	(Rd 4) Swansea	(h)	3-0
(Toshack, St John, Lawler; 47,229)			
Feb 13	(Rd 5) Southampton	(h)	1-0
(Lawler; 50,226)			
Mar 6	(Rd 6) Tottenham	(h)	0-0
(54,731)			
Mar 16	(replay) Tottenham	(a)	1-0
(Heighway; 56,283)			
Mar 27	(SF) Everton (Old Trafford)	(n)	2-1
(Evans, Hall; 62,144)			
May 8	(F) Arsenal (W = Wembley)	(W)	1-2
(Heighway, after extra time; 100,000)			

FA Cup goalscorers: Heighway 2, Lawler 2, Evans, McLaughlin, Toshack, St John, Hall

Fairs Cup

Sep 15	(Rd 1, 1st leg) Ferencvaros	(h)	1-0
(Graham; 37,531)			
Sep 29	(Rd 1, 2nd leg) Ferencvaros	(a)	1-1
(Hughes; 25,000)			
Oct 21	(RD 2, 1st leg) D Bucharest	(h)	3-0
(Lindsay, Lawler, Hughes; 36,525)			
Nov 4	(Rd 2, 2nd leg) D Bucharest	(a)	1-1
(Boersma; 50,000)			
Dec 9	(Rd 3, 1st leg) Hibernian	(a)	1-0
(Toshack; 30,296)			
Dec 22	(Rd 3, 2nd leg) Hibernian	(h)	2-0
(Heighway, Boersma; 37,815)			
Mar 10	(Rd 4, 1st leg) Bayern Munich	(h)	3-0
(Evans 3; 45,616)			
Mar 24	(Rd 4, 2nd leg) Bayern Munich	(a)	1-1
(Ross; 23,000)			
Apr 14	(SF 1st leg) Leeds	(h)	0-1
(52,877)			
Apr 28	(SF 2nd leg) Leeds	(a)	0-0
(40,462)			

Fairs Cup goalscorers: Evans 3, Hughes 2, Boersma 2, Graham, Heighway, Lindsay, Lawler, Toshack, Ross

1971-2

By Liverpool's immensely high standards, the season was a disaster. Not one trophy came to Anfield and the Reds were knocked out of their three knockout cups in the very early stages. Yet there were plenty of things to smile about as Kevin Keegan made an early impact on the First Division, scoring on his debut and finishing the season as second-highest scorer (albeit with just nine goals) to John Toshack.

Keegan was signed from Scunthorpe as a midfield player and when Liverpool went on a close season tour to Scandinavia, the youngster was used as such — playing with the number eight shirt on his back in a kind of defensive winger role. Yet even with this restriction on him, Keegan still managed to score two goals and when the party arrived back at Anfield, Keegan was played in the attack for a few practice games — during which time he scored a hat-trick against the club's reserve side which had won the Central League championship for the previous three seasons. And when Nottingham Forest came to Liverpool for the first match of the season, Keegan was in the Liverpool side wearing the number seven shirt.

Nearly 51,000 Anfield fans saw Keegan score Liverpool's first goal as they went on to win 3-1, and by the end of the season, Liverpool's new star had played in thirty-five league matches. Yet Keegan's recall to the side in December coincided with one of the leanest patches that the club has endured in recent seasons. After beating Derby 3-2 on 11 December, Liverpool went five league matches without scoring a goal, during which time they lost three times. It was a spell which undoubtedly cost them the championship because when they came to their last game of the season, Liverpool needed an away win to clinch the title which should have been sewn up weeks before.

Liverpool's penultimate league match had been at Derby on 1 May where John McGovern's goal gave Brian Clough's side a 1-0 win and put them on top of the First Division. It was Derby's last game and with both Leeds (away to Wolves) and Liverpool (away to Arsenal) still to play, the title did not look as if it was heading for the Baseball Ground. But both Liverpool and Leeds fell; Leeds needed to draw, but lost; and Liverpool were in need of two points but could only manage a goalless draw at Highbury. Thus, Derby players learned that they were champions while they were sunning themselves in Majorca, far away from the battlefields of the First Division. Apart from everything else, Liverpool looked back to that five-match spell at the turn of the year, knowing that just one goal in 450 minutes football would have left them under less pressure at Highbury. The championship had already been lost by then.

Leicester's Peter Shilton can only look sick as Keegan and Toshack celebrate a Liverpool goal at Anfield in August 1971.

First Division results 1971-2

Aug 14 Nottm Forest .... (h) 3-1
(Keegan, Smith pen, Hughes; 50,989)
Aug 17 Wolves .... (h) 3-2
(Toshack, Heighway, Smith pen; 51,869)
Aug 21 Newcastle .... (a) 2-3
(Hughes, Keegan; 39,720)
Aug 24 Crystal Palace .... (a) 1-0
(Toshack; 28,488)
Aug 28 Leicester .... (h) 3-2
(Heighway, Keegan, Toshack; 50,970)
Sep 1   Man City .... (a) 0-1
(45,144)
Sep 4   Tottenham .... (a) 0-2
(50,124)
Sep 11 Southampton .... (h) 1-0
(Toshack; 45,876)
Sep 18 Leeds .... (a) 0-1
(41,381)
Sep 25 Man United .... (h) 2-2
(Graham, Hall; 55,634)
Oct 2   Stoke .... (a) 0-0
(28,698)
Oct 9   Chelsea .... (h) 0-0
(48,464)
Oct 16 Nottm Forest .... (a) 3-2
(Hughes, Heighway, Smith pen; 20,945)
Oct 23 Huddersfield .... (h) 2-0
(Smith pen, Evans; 41,627)
Oct 30 Sheffield United ..... (a) 1-1
(Keegan; 39,023)
Nov 6   Arsenal .... (h) 3-2
(Hughes, Callaghan, Ross; 46,929)
Nov 13 Everton .... (a) 0-1
(56,563)
Nov 20 Coventry .... (a) 2-0
(Whitham 2; 25,325)
Nov 27 West Ham .... (h) 1-0
(Hughes; 43,399)
Dec 4   Ipswich .... (a) 0-0
(21,359)
Dec 11 Derby .... (h) 3-2
(Whitham 3; 44,601)
Dec 18 Tottenham .... (h) 0-0
(43,409)
Dec 27 West Brom .... (a) 0-1
(43,804)
Jan 1   Leeds .... (h) 0-2
(53,847)
Jan 8   Leicester .... (a) 0-1
(26,421)
Jan 22 Wolves .... (a) 0-0
(33,638)
Jan 29 Crystal Palace .... (h) 4-1
(Callaghan, Lawler 2, Keegan; 39,538)
Feb 12 Huddersfield .... (a) 1-0
(Whitham; 18,702)
Feb 19 Sheffield United ..... (h) 2-0
(Toshack 2; 42,005)
Feb 26 Man City .... (h) 3-0
(Lloyd, Keegan, Graham; 50,074)
Mar 4   Everton .... (h) 4-0
(Lawler, Hughes, own goals 2; 53,922)
Mar 11 Chelsea .... (a) 0-0
(38,691)
Mar 18 Newcastle .... (h) 5-0
(Lawler, Toshack, Keegan, Hughes, Boersma; 43,899)
Mar 25 Southampton .... (a) 1-0
(Toshack; 21,680)
Mar 28 Stoke .... (h) 2-1
(Keegan, opp own goal; 42,489)
Apr 1   West Brom .... (h) 2-0
(Smith pen, Lawler; 46,564)
Apr 3   Man United .... (a) 3-0
(Lawler, Toshack, Hughes; 54,000)
Apr 8   Coventry .... (h) 3-1
(Keegan, Smith pen, Toshack; 50,628)
Apr 15 West Ham .... (a) 2-0
(Toshack, Heighway; 32,660)
Apr 22 Ipswich .... (h) 2-0
(Toshack 2; 54,316)
May 1   Derby .... (a) 0-1
(39,420)
May 8   Arsenal .... (a) 0-0
(39,289)

Final League record

P	W	D	L	F	A	Pts	Pos
42	24	9	9	64	30	57	3rd

Football League goalscorers: Toshack 13, Keegan 9, Hughes 8, Smith 6, Whitham 6, Lawler 6, Heighway 4, Graham 2, Callaghan 2, Boersma, Hall, Evans, Ross, Lloyd, own goals 3

Keegan scores the first of Liverpool's three goals against Coventry at Anfield on April 8 1972.

Allan Clarke's two goals sunk Liverpool's hopes of a return to Wembley in the FA Cup when Leeds won their fourth round replay 2-0 at Elland Road; and in the fourth round of the League Cup, Geoff Hurst and Pop Robson hit Liverpool at Upton Park to seal off their chances of a Wembley place via the competition which the Reds had, for so long, ignored. With Arsenal's 'double' of the previous season, Liverpool found themselves in the Cup-winners Cup, despite the fact that the trophy was at Highbury, not Anfield, but here again they failed. Bayern Munich exacted revenge by holding Liverpool 0-0 on Merseyside and then winning 3-1 in Bavaria to complete a barren season for the Reds. It was, however, an unfair reflection on a season when Liverpool's team had played superbly for much of the time.

FA Cup

Jan 15 (Rd 3) Oxford Utd..... (a) 3-0
(Keegan 2, Lindsay; 18,000)
Feb 5 (Rd 4) Leeds.......... (h) 0-0
(56,300)
Feb 9 (replay) Leeds......... (a) 0-2
(45,821)
FA Cup goalscorers: Keegan 2, Lindsay

Football League Cup

Sep 7 (Rd 2) Hull........... (h) 3-0
(Lawler, Heighway, Hall pen; 31,612)
Oct 5 (Rd 3) Southampton ... (h) 1-0
(Heighway; 29,964)
Oct 26 (Rd 4) West Ham ..... (a) 1-2
(Graham; 40,878)
Football League Cup goalscorers: Heighway 2, Hall, Graham, Lawler

Cup-winners Cup

Sep 15 (Rd 1, 1st leg) Servette . (a) 1-2
(Lawler; 20,000)
Sep 29 (Rd 1, 2nd leg) Servette (h) 2-0
(Hughes, Heighway; 38,591)
Oct 20 (Rd 2, 1st leg) Bayern
            Munich................ (h) 0-0
(42,949)
Nov 3 (Rd 2, 2nd leg) Bayern
            Munich................ (a) 1-3
(Evans; 40,000)
Cup-winners Cup goalscorers: Hughes, Heighway, Evans, Lawler

Liverpool v Ipswich, 22 April 1972. David Best clears from Toshack and Heighway.

1972-3

No trophies in 1971-2 meant that Bill Shankly's men had a lot to put right in 1972-3 — and how they responded! First Division champions and UEFA Cup winners, as well as reaching the quarter-finals of the Football League Cup was enough to satisfy the appetites of even Liverpool's loyal thousands. Liverpool finished three points ahead of Arsenal and seven points clear of Leeds United, with previous champions, Derby, slumping down to seventh in the First Division table.

Liverpool lost only seven matches and Keegan played in all but one league game, joining Toshack on thirteen goals to become the Reds' joint-leading scorer. Yet Liverpool often left things until very late in their game; nine times the Reds scored the winning goal in the last five minutes to make First Division defences realise that they could not afford to let up on Liverpool, not even for a split second. The FA Cup proved a disappointment when Liverpool could only draw with Manchester City in their fourth round clash at Anfield and in the Maine Road replay, Bell and Booth scored the goals which ended Anfield's Wembley dreams for another season. In the League Cup Liverpool battled through to the fifth round before Spurs drew at Anfield and in the replay at White Hart Lane, Martin Chivers (2) and John Pratt sunk the Reds 3-1.

Liverpool had more than ample revenge against Tottenham when the teams met again in the semi-final of the UEFA Cup. Alec Lindsay gave Liverpool a 1-0 win in the first-leg at Anfield and the Reds went to London, knowing that they had to score a vital away goal to put the tie beyond doubt. It was a fact that Liverpool had to score when Martin Peters equalised early in the second half, and Steve Heighway netted the vital goal soon after. Although Peters made the score 2-1 on the night, and although the Spurs man also hit the Liverpool woodwork, Liverpool, went through to the UEFA Cup Final by virtue of Heighway's goal which counted double away from home.

Liverpool v AEK Athens (UEFA Cup 2nd round, first leg at Anfield, 24 October 1972). Chris Lawler is foiled by the Greek goalkeeper.

Liverpool met West Germany's Borussia Moenchengladbach on a home and away basis, but only half-an-hour of the first-leg at Anfield had been played when the referee halted play because torrential rain had made the Liverpool pitch unplayable. When the teams tried again, Shankly, wise old fox that he is, thought back to that first abortive game and brought in John Toshack for the hard-working Hall. After thirty-three minutes Toshack had twice flicked the ball on for Keegan to score and Liverpool were coasting home. Ray Clemence saved a penalty and Larry Lloyd made the final scoreline 3-0 — a handsome lead for Liverpool to take to Dusseldorf. It was as well that Liverpool had opened up such a big lead. Gunter Netzer inspired Borussia to a 2-0 win to leave Liverpool holders of the UEFA Cup with a single goal separating the two sides. It was a great night for Liverpool with thousands of red-and-white bedecked supporters, together with hundreds of British soldiers and airmen, joining together in the song which has become Liverpool's battle hymn — *You'll Never Walk Alone*. Indeed, Liverpool's travels through Europe have never been alone.

Larry Lloyd scores Liverpool's third goal in the first leg of the UEFA Cup Final against Borussia Moechengladbach.

First Division results 1972-3

Date	Opponent	H/A	Score
Aug 12	Man City	(h)	2-0
	(Hall, Callaghan; 55,383)		
Aug 15	Man United	(h)	2-0
	(Toshack, Heighway; 54,779)		
Aug 19	Crystal Palace	(a)	1-1
	(Hughes; 30,054)		
Aug 23	Chelsea	(a)	2-1
	(Toshack, Callaghan; 35,375)		
Aug 26	West Ham	(h)	3-2
	(Toshack, Hughes, opp own goal; 50,491)		
Aug 30	Leicester	(a)	2-3
	(Toshack 2; 28,694)		
Sep 2	Derby	(a)	1-2
	(Toshack; 32,524)		
Sep 9	Wolves	(h)	4-2
	(Hughes, Cormack, Smith pen, Keegan; 43,386)		
Sep 16	Arsenal	(a)	0-0
	(47,597)		
Sep 23	Sheffield United	(h)	5-0
	(Boersma, Cormack, Lindsay, Heighway, Keegan pen; 42,940)		
Sep 30	Leeds	(a)	2-1
	(Lloyd, Boersma; 46,468)		
Oct 7	Everton	(h)	1-0
	(Cormack; 55,975)		
Oct 14	Southampton	(a)	1-1
	(Lawler; 24,100)		
Oct 21	Stoke	(h)	2-1
	(Hughes, Callaghan; 45,604)		
Oct 28	Norwich	(a)	1-0
	(Cormack; 36,625)		
Nov 4	Chelsea	(h)	3-1
	(Toshack 2, Keegan; 48,932)		
Nov 11	Man United	(a)	0-2
	(53,944)		
Nov 18	Newcastle	(h)	3-2
	(Cormack, Lindsay, Toshack; 46,153)		
Nov 25	Tottenham	(a)	2-1
	(Heighway, Keegan; 45,399)		
Dec 2	Birmingham	(h)	4-3
	(Lindsay 2, Cormack, Toshack; 45,407)		
Dec 9	West Brom	(a)	1-1
	(Boersma; 32,000)		
Dec 16	Ipswich	(a)	1-1
	(Heighway; 25,693)		
Dec 23	Coventry	(h)	2-0
	(Toshack 2; 41,550)		
Dec 26	Sheffield United	(a)	3-0
	(Boersma, Lawler, Heighway; 34,040)		
Dec 30	Crystal Palace	(h)	1-0
	(Cormack; 50,862)		
Jan 6	West Ham	(a)	1-0
	(Keegan; 34,480)		
Jan 20	Derby	(h)	1-1
	(Toshack; 45,996)		
Jan 27	Wolves	(a)	1-2
	(Keegan; 32,957)		

Feb 10	Arsenal	(h)	0-2
(49,898)
| Feb 17 | Man City | (a) | 1-1 |
(Boersma; 40,528)
| Feb 24 | Ipswich | (h) | 2-1 |
(Heighway, Keegan; 43,875)
| Mar 3 | Everton | (a) | 2-0 |
(Hughes 2; 54,269)
| Mar 10 | Southampton | (h) | 3-2 |
(Lloyd, Keegan 2; 41,674)
| Mar 17 | Stoke | (a) | 1-0 |
(opp own goal; 33,540)
| Mar 24 | Norwich | (h) | 3-1 |
(Lawler, Hughes, Hall; 42,995)
| Mar 31 | Tottenham | (h) | 1-1 |
(Keegan; 48,477)
| Apr 7 | Birmingham | (a) | 1-2 |
(Smith; 48,114)
| Apr 14 | West Brom | (h) | 1-0 |
(Keegan pen; 43,853)
| Apr 17 | Coventry | (a) | 2-1 |
(Boersma 2; 27,280)
| Apr 21 | Newcastle | (a) | 1-2 |
(Keegan; 37,240)
| Apr 23 | Leeds | (h) | 2-0 |
(Cormack, Keegan; 55,738)
| Apr 28 | Leicester | (h) | 0-0 |
(56,202)

Final League record

P	W	D	L	F	A	Pts	Pos
42	25	10	7	72	42	60	1st

Football League goalscorers: Toshack 13, Keegan 13, Cormack 8, Hughes 7, Boersma 7, Heighway 6, Lindsay 4, Callaghan 3, Lawler 3, Hall 2, Smith 2, Lloyd 2, own goals 2

FA Cup

Jan 13	(Rd 3)	Burnley	(a)	0-0
(35,730)
| Jan 16 | (replay) | Burnley | (h) | 3-0 |
(Toshack 2, Cormack; 56,124)
| Feb 3 | (Rd 4) Man City | (h) | 0-0 |
(56,296)
| Feb 7 | (replay) | Man City | (a) | 0-2 |
(49,572)

FA Cup goalscorers: Toshack 2, Cormack

Football League Cup

Sep 5	(Rd 2)	Carlisle	(a)	1-1
(Keegan; 16,257)
| Sep 19 | (replay) | Carlisle | (h) | 5-1 |
(Keegan, Boersma 2, Lawler, Heighway; 22,182)
| Oct 3 | (Rd 3) | West Brom | (a) | 1-1 |
(Heighway; 17,756)
| Oct 10 | (replay) | West Brom | (h) | 2-1 |
(Hughes, Keegan after extra time; 26,461)
| Oct 31 | (Rd 4) | Leeds | (h) | 2-2 |
(Keegan, Toshack; 44,609)
| Nov 22 | (replay) | Leeds | (a) | 1-0 |
(Keegan; 34,856)
| Dec 4 | (Rd 5) | Tottenham | (h) | 1-1 |
(Hughes; 48,677)
| Dec 6 | (replay) | Tottenham | (a) | 1-3 |
(Callaghan; 34,565)

Football League Cup goalscorers: Keegan 5, Heighway 2, Boersma 2, Hughes 2, Lawler, Callaghan, Toshack

UEFA Cup

Sep 12	(Rd 1, 1st leg) E Frankfurt	(h)	2-0
(Keegan, Hughes; 33,380)
| Sep 26 | (Rd 1, 2nd leg) E Frankfurt | (a) | 0-0 |
(18,000)
| Oct 24 | (Rd 2, 1st leg) AEK Athens | (h) | 3-0 |
(Cormack, Boersma, Smith pen; 31,906)
| Nov 11 | (Rd 2, 2nd leg) AEK Athens | (a) | 3-1 |
(Hughes 2, Boersma; 25,000)
| Nov 29 | (Rd 3, 1st leg) Dynamo Berlin | (a) | 0-0 |
(20,000)
| Dec 12 | (Rd 3, 2nd leg) Dynamo Berlin | (h) | 3-1 |
(Boersma, Heighway, Toshack; 34,140)
| Mar 7 | (QF 1st leg) Dynamo Dresden | (h) | 2-0 |
(Hall, Boersma; 33,270)
| Mar 21 | (QF 2nd leg) Dynamo Dresden | (a) | 1-0 |
(Keegan; 35,000)
| Apr 10 | (SF 1st leg) Tottenham | (h) | 1-0 |
(Lindsay; 42,174)
| Apr 23 | (SF 2nd leg) Tottenham | (a) | 1-2 |
(Heighway; 46,919) Liverpool won on away goals rule
| May 10 | (Final 1st leg) Borussia Moen | (h) | 3-0 |
(Keegan 2, Lloyd; 41,169)
| May 23 | (Final 2nd leg) Borussia Moen | (a) | 0-2 |
(35,000)

UEFA Cup goalscorers: Boersma 4, Keegan 4, Hughes 3, Heighway 2, Cormack 1, Smith 1, Toshack 1, Hall 1, Lindsay 1, Lloyd 1

1973-4

Although they missed out on a second successive First Division championship by finishing five points behind the eventual title holders, Leeds United, and although their European Cup quest was over by the second round, Liverpool still made their mark on this season by winning the FA Cup against Newcastle United at Wembley. It seemed as though Liverpool simply fell at one hurdle — and then just picked themselves up and climbed over another.

All eyes at Anfield were set on the European Cup but even in their first round match against the part-timers of Luxembourg's champions, Jeunesse D'Esch, Liverpool did not have things all their own way and the minnows held the English giants 1-1 in Luxembourg and battled all the way at Anfield before going down 2-0. In the second round Liverpool could be pleased with a 2-1 defeat at the hands of Red Star Belgrade in Yugoslavia, where Chris Lawler gave them a priceless away goal which meant that a 1-0 victory at Anfield would see the Reds through. But Red Star's coach Miljan Miljanic — the man who later went to Real Madrid and who Chelsea wanted to revitalise their own flagging fortunes — promised that Red Star would attack at Anfield and this they did, winning 2-1 again to put Liverpool out of the European Cup before their own shocked supporters.

Liverpool made the quarter-finals of the Football League Cup, though not before Hull City had forced mighty Reds to a replay where Ian Callaghan's hat-trick finally knocked out the Tigers of Boothferry Park. In the fifth round Liverpool faced another challenge in old gold — this time not Tigers, but Wolves. There were less than 16,000 fans at Molineux to watch John Richards score the only goal of the game to put Wolves a stage nearer the final.

It was the FA Cup which finally saw Liverpool 'come good' in 1973-4. In the third round Kevin Keegan went back to the lower divisions and scored the two goals which earned Liverpool a 2-2 draw in a surprisingly difficult tie at Doncaster Rovers. Even at Anfield, Liverpool failed to deliver a hammer blow to a team separated from them by eighty-odd league placings, but the Reds 2-0 win was good enough to put them against Carlisle United in the fourth round. Again, Liverpool struggled against a team from a lower division — this time the Second — and Carlisle forced a goalless draw before they, too, lost 2-0 at Anfield. Liverpool had less difficulty in beating Ipswich Town and Bristol City and they faced Leicester in the semi-final.

Keegan about to turn the ball into the Newcastle net during the 1974 FA Cup Final.

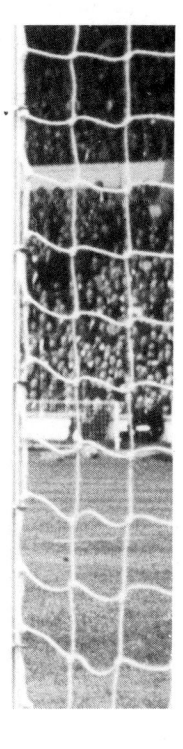

A third tie going to a replay faced Liverpool before they disposed of Leicester at the second attempt, drawing 0-0 at Old Trafford before Villa Park's 55,000 saw Hall, Keegan and Toshack swamp the Filbert Street club for the Reds to win 3-1. They met Newcastle United in the Wembley final on 4 May 1974, after Newcastle had beaten Burnley 2-0 at Hillsborough. Newcastle were never in the hunt in the 1974 FA Cup Final. On Wembley's wide, open spaces, Liverpool dominated the match and gave the Newcastle defenders in particular, a nightmare of an afternoon. Kevin Keegan struck home two goals — one, after a move involving most of the Liverpool team — and Steve Heighway netted the other as the Reds won 3-0 to take the trophy back to Merseyside where a quarter-of-a-million ecstatic fans paid homage to their gods.

First Division results 1973-4

Aug 25 Stoke .... (h) 1-0
(Heighway; 52,935)
Aug 28 Coventry .... (a) 0-1
(29,305)
Sep 1 Leicester .... (a) 1-1
(Toshack; 29,347)
Sep 4 Derby .... (h) 2-0
(Thompson, Keegan pen; 45,237)
Sep 8 Chelsea .... (h) 1-0
(Keegan; 47,016)
Sep 12 Derby .... (a) 1-3
(Boersma; 32,867)
Sep 15 Birmingham .... (a) 1-1
(Hall; 35,719)
Sep 22 Tottenham .... (h) 3-2
(Lawler 2, Lindsay pen; 42,901)
Sep 29 Man United .... (a) 0-0
(53,882)
Oct 6 Newcastle .... (h) 2-1
(Cormack, Lindsay pen; 45,612)
Oct 13 Southampton .... (a) 0-1
(22,018)
Oct 20 Leeds .... (a) 0-1
(44,911)
Oct 27 Sheffield United .... (h) 1-0
(Keegan; 40,641)
Nov 3 Arsenal .... (a) 2-0
(Hughes, Toshack; 39,837)
Nov 10 Wolves .... (h) 1-0
(Heighway; 38,088)
Nov 17 Ipswich .... (h) 4-2
(Keegan 3, Cormack; 37,420)
Nov 24 QPR .... (a) 2-2
(Lloyd, Toshack; 26,254)
Dec 1 West Ham .... (h) 1-0
(Cormack; 34,857)
Dec 8 Everton .... (a) 1-0
(Waddle; 56,098)
Dec 15 Norwich .... (a) 1-1
(Cormack; 20,628)
Dec 22 Man United .... (h) 2-0
(Keegan, Heighway; 40,420)
Dec 26 Burnley .... (a) 1-2
(Cormack; 24,404)
Dec 29 Chelsea .... (a) 1-0
(Cormack; 32,901)
Jan 1 Leicester .... (h) 1-1
(Cormack; 39,110)
Jan 12 Birmingham .... (h) 3-2
(Keegan 2, Thompson; 39,094)
Jan 19 Stoke .... (a) 1-1
(Smith; 32,789)
Feb 2 Norwich .... (h) 1-0
(Cormack; 31,742)
Feb 5 Coventry .... (h) 2-1
(Lindsay pen, Keegan; 21,656)
Feb 23 Newcastle .... (a) 0-0
(41,727)
Feb 26 Southampton .... (h) 1-0
(Boersma; 27,105)
Mar 2 Burnley .... (h) 1-0
(Toshack; 42,562)
Mar 16 Leeds .... (h) 1-0
(Heighway; 56,003)
Mar 23 Wolves .... (a) 1-0
(Hall; 35,867)
Apr 6 QPR .... (h) 2-1
(Lindsay pen, opp own goal; 54,027)
Apr 8 Sheffield Utd .... (a) 0-1
(31,809)
Apr 12 Man City .... (a) 1-1
(Cormack; 43,284)
Apr 13 Ipswich .... (a) 1-1
(Hughes; 33,285)
Apr 16 Man City .... (h) 4-0
(Hall 2, Boersma, Keegan; 50,781)
Apr 20 Everton .... (h) 0-0
(55,858)
Apr 24 Arsenal .... (h) 0-1
(47,997)
Apr 27 West Ham .... (a) 2-2
(Toshack, Keegan; 36,160)
May 8 Tottenham .... (a) 1-1
(Heighway; 24,718)

Final League record

P	W	D	L	F	A	Pts	Pos
42	22	13	7	52	31	57	2nd

Football League goalscorers: Keegan 12, Cormack 9, Heighway 5, Toshack 5, Hall 4, Lindsay 4, Boersma 3, Thompson 2, Lawler 2, Hughes 2, Lloyd 1, Waddle 1, Smith 1, own goals 1

FA Cup

Jan 5	(Rnd 3)	Doncaster	(h)	2-2

(Keegan 2; 31,483)

Jan 8	(replay)	Doncaster	(a)	2-0

(Heighway, Cormack; 22,499)

Jan 26	(Rnd 4)	Carlisle	(h)	0-0

(47,211)

Jan 29	(replay)	Carlisle	(a)	2-0

(Boersma, Toshack; 21,262)

Feb 16	(Rnd 5)	Ipswich	(h)	2-0

(Hall, Keegan; 45,340)

Mar 9	(Rnd 6)	Bristol City	(a)	1-0

(Toshack; 37,671)

Mar 30	(SF)	Leicester	MU	0-0

(MU = Man Utd)
(60,000)

Apr 3	(replay)	Leicester	V	3-1

(V = Villa)
(Hall, Keegan, Toshack; 55,619)

May 4	(Final)	Newcastle	W	3-0

(W = Wembley)
(Keegan 2, Heighway; 100,000)

FA Cup goalscorers: Keegan 6, Toshack 3, Hall 2, Heighway 2, Cormack, Boersma

Football League Cup

Oct 8	(Rnd 2)	West Ham	(a)	2-2

(Cormack, Heighway; 25,840)

Oct 29	(replay)	West Ham	(h)	1-0

(Toshack; 26,002)

Nov 21	(Rnd 3)	Sunderland	(a)	2-0

(Keegan, Toshack; 36,208)

Nov 27	(Rnd 4)	Hull	(a)	0-0

(19,748)

Dec 4	(replay)	Hull	(h)	3-1

(Callaghan 3; 17,120)

Dec 19	(Rnd 2)	Wolves	(a)	0-1

(15,242)

Football League Cup goalscorers: Callaghan 3, Toshack 2, Cormack 1, Heighway 1, Keegan 1

European Cup

Sep 19	(Rnd 1, 1st leg)

Jeunesse D'Esch .... (a) 1-1
(Hall; 7,000)

Oct 3 (Rnd 1, 2nd leg)
Jeunesse D'Esch .... (h) 2-0
(Toshack, opp own goal; 28,714)

Oct 24 (Rnd 2, 1st leg)
Red Star Belgrade .. (a) 1-2
(Lawler; 30,000)

Nov 6 (Rnd 2, 2nd leg)
Red Star Belgrade .. (h) 1-2
(Lawler; 41,774)

European Cup goalscorers: Lawler 2, Hall 1, Toshack 1, own goal 1

Brian Hall scored twice as Liverpool beat Manchester City 4-1 on Boxing Day 1974.

1974-5

Bill Shankly went out and bought Arsenal's £200,000 striker, Ray Kennedy, in yet another astute piece of business — and then dropped the bombshell that he was to retire from football. Soccer without Shankly was unthinkable. For over forty years — as player and manager — the Scot had breathed life and fire into the game. His own inimitable brand of fervour, dedication and absolute commitment had rubbed off on players, supporters and directors alike. Now he wanted a rest. At first, the Liverpool Board of Directors tried hard to persuade Shankly to change his mind. They offered him a new contract — and he could name his own terms — but money was not the thing which motivated the old Anfield tiger. Bill Shankly had made up his mind that he wanted a break from the game he had graced for so long — and there was nothing that the Liverpool club could do about it except look round for a successor. They did not have far to look. Shankly's assistant, Bob Paisley, would ensure that the Liverpool dynasty remained. There were certain difficulties to begin with — only inevitable when the man who *was* Liverpool Football Club decided to stand down — but the transfer of power was relatively smooth and meant that Liverpool would not suffer the fate of many clubs in having wholesale changes sweeping through their organisation with a change of manager. It was Shankly's own idea that Paisley, together with the coaching staff of Joe Fagan, Reuben Bennett, Ron Moran, Roy Evans and Tom Saunders should all move up.

Liverpool failed to win anything in 1974-5, finishing runners-up in the First Division to Derby and failing in the FA, League and Cup-winners Cups. In the league they were never lower than sixth place — after Derby beat them 2-0 at the Baseball Ground on 11 January — and they finally finished two points adrift, thanks to a 1-0 defeat at Middlesbrough in the penultimate match of the season when Alan Foggon scored the goal which probably decided where the title was destined for.

In the FA Cup, Ipswich Town's Mick Mills scored the only goal of the fourth round tie at Portman Road to bring Liverpool crashing down; and it was at Ayrsome Park, Middlesbrough where a lone goal also saw an end to Liverpool's League Cup hopes when Bill Maddren's effort beat Liverpool 1-0.

The Reds had found goals in plentiful supply in the Cup-winners Cup when they chalked up a record club win of 11-0 against the Norwegian Cup winners, Stromgodset. Nine different players went on the scoresheet that night and 17,000 Norwegians saw the English Cup holders win 1-0 in Norway through Ray Kennedy. But Liverpool were to proceed no further. The Hungarians of Ferencvaros beat them after two drawn games — Ferencvaros going through by virtue of their away goal in the 1-1 draw at Anfield — and Liverpool were out.

First Division results 1974-5

Aug 17 Luton .... (a) 2-1
(Smith, Heighway; 21,062)
Aug 20 Wolves .... (a) 0-0
(33,499)
Aug 24 Leicester .... (h) 2-1
(Lindsay 2 pens; 49,398)
Aug 27 Wolves .... (h) 2-0
(Heighway, Toshack; 42,449)
Aug 31 Chelsea .... (a) 3-0
(Kennedy, Boersma 2; 39,461)
Sep 7   Tottenham .... (h) 5-2
(Boersma 3, Hughes, Kennedy; 47,538)
Sep 14 Man City .... (a) 0-2
(45,194)
Sep 21 Stoke .... (h) 3-0
(Boersma, Heighway, opp own goal; 51,423)
Sep 24 Burnley .... (h) 0-1
(44,639)
Sep 28 Sheffield Utd ...... (a) 0-1
(29,443)
Oct 5   Carlisle .... (a) 1-0
(Kennedy; 20,844)
Oct 12 Middlesbrough ...... (h) 2-0
(Callaghan, Keegan pen; 52,590)
Oct 19 QPR .... (a) 1-0
(Hall; 27,392)
Oct 26 Leeds .... (h) 1-0
(Heighway; 54,996)
Nov 2   Ipswich .... (a) 0-1
(30,564)
Nov 9   Arsenal .... (h) 1-3
(Kennedy; 43,850)
Nov 16 Everton .... (a) 0-0
(56,797)
Nov 23 West Ham .... (h) 1-1
(Smith; 46,346)
Nov 30 Coventry .... (a) 1-1
(Keegan; 23,089)
Dec 7   Derby .... (h) 2-2
(Kennedy, Heighway; 41,058)
Dec 14 Luton .... (h) 2-0
(Toshack, Heighway; 35,151)

Dec 21   Birmingham ....   (a)   1-3
(Toshack; 26,608)
Dec 26   Man City ....   (h)   4-1
(Hall 2, Toshack, Heighway; 46,062)
Jan 11   Derby ....   (a)   0-2
(33,463)
Jan 18   Coventry ....   (h)   2-1
(Heighway, Keegan; 43,668)
Feb 1   Arsenal ....   (a)   0-2
(43,028)
Feb 8   Ipswich ....   (h)   5-2
(Hall, Toshack 2, Lindsay, Cormack; 47,421)
Feb 15   Newcastle ....   (a)   1-4
(Hall; 38,115)
Feb 19   West Ham ....   (a)   0-0
(40,256)
Feb 22   Everton ....   (h)   0-0
(55,853)
Mar 1   Chelsea ....   (h)   2-2
(Heighway, Cormack; 42,726)
Mar 8   Burnley ....   (a)   1-1
(McDermott; 31,812)
Mar 15   Sheffield United ......   (h)   0-0
(40,862)
Mar 19   Leicester ....   (a)   1-1
(Toshack; 28,012)
Mar 22   Tottenham ....   (a)   2-0
(Keegan, Cormack; 34,331)
Mar 25   Newcastle ....   (h)   4-0
(Keegan, Toshack 2, McDermott; 41,147)
Mar 29   Birmingham ....   (h)   1-0
(Keegan pen; 49,454)
Mar 31   Stoke ....   (a)   0-2
(45,594)
Apr 5   Leeds ....   (a)   2-0
(Keegan 2; 34,971)
Apr 12   Carlisle ....   (h)   2-0
(Toshack, Keegan; 46,073)
Apr 19   Middlesborough ....   (a)   0-1
(34,027)
Apr 26   QPR ....   (h)   3-1
(Toshack 2, Keegan pen; 42,546)

Final League record

P	W	D	L	F	A	Pts	Pos
42	20	11	11	60	39	51	2nd

Football League goalscorers: Toshack 12, Keegan 10, Heighway 9, Boersma 6, Kennedy 5, Hall 5, Lindsay 3, Cormack 3, Smith 2, McDermott 2, Hughes 1, Callaghan 1, opp own goal 1

FA Cup

Jan 3   (Rnd 3)   Stoke ....   (h)   2-0
(Heighway, Keegan; 48,723)
Jan 24   (Rnd 4)   Ipswich ....   (a)   0-1
(34,709)
FA Cup goalscorers: Heighway, Keegan

Football League Cup

Sep 10   (Rnd 2)   Brentford   (h)   2-1
(Kennedy, Boersma; 21,413)
Oct 8   (Rnd 3)   Bristol City .... (a)   0-0
(25,573)
Oct 16   (replay) Bristol City   (h)   4-0
(Heighway 2, Kennedy 2; 23,694)
Nov 12   (Rnd 4)   Middlesbrough. (h)   0-1
(24,906)
Football League Cup goalscorers: Kennedy 3, Heighway 2, Boersma 1

Cup-winners Cup

Sep 17   (Rnd 1, 1st leg)
         Stromgodset ....   (h)   11-0
(Lindsay pen, Boersma 2, Thompson 2, Heighway 1, Cormack 1, Hughes 1, Callaghan 1, Smith 1, Kennedy 1; 24,743)
Oct 1   (Rnd 1, 2nd leg)
         Stromgodset ....   (a)   1-0
(Kennedy; 17,000)
Oct 23   (Rnd 2, 1st leg)
         Ferencvaros ....   (h)   1-1
(Keegan; 35,027)
Nov 5   (Rnd 2, 2nd leg)
         Ferencvaros ....   (a)   0-0
(30,000) Liverpool lost on away goals rule.
Cup-winners Cup goalscorers: Boersma 2, Thompson 2, Kennedy 2, Keegan 1, Smith 1, Callaghan 1, Hughes 1, Cormack 1, Heighway 1, Lindsay 1

Phil Thompson hit two as Liverpool rattled up eleven goals against the Norwegians of Stromgodset.

1975-6

It did not take Bob Paisley long to take up where Bill Shankly had left off. The former Liverpool wing-half guided them to the First Division championship again and also put Liverpool's hold back on the UEFA Cup which they had won three seasons earlier. Again, there were disappointments in the two domestic cup competitions, but to dwell on those is to take away the real significance of a season which saw Anfield finally take a grip on English — and European — football.

Liverpool had, in fact, started badly when Gerry Francis and Mike Leach gave Queen's Park Rangers a 2-0 win at Loftus Road on the opening day of the season; then West Ham United managed a 2-2 draw in midweek — Liverpool's first home match — and by the time Spurs came to Anfield for the second Saturday of the new campaign, Liverpool were in the bottom half of the table. But Spurs went away, whipped 3-2 and from that moment, Liverpool climbed steadily up the First Division until on 20 December, Queen's Park Rangers came to Anfield for the return fixture and a 2-0 win by the Reds put them on top of the league. The Reds lost only two more games — away to Arsenal, and at home to their 'bogey' team, Middlesbrough — and they were never out of the top four, finally clinching the title with a 3-1 win at Wolves in the last match of the season. Liverpool were trailing 1-0 at half-time but Keegan, Toshack and Kennedy struck second half goals that left them one point clear of QPR.

The UEFA Cup trail started disappointingly when Hibernian beat Liverpool 1-0 in Edinburgh in the first-leg — and Ray Clemence saved a penalty at that — before John Toshack's marvellous hat-trick at Anfield Road more than compensated, leaving Liverpool 3-2 aggregate winners. The Reds found goals aplenty in the next round when they hit the Spaniards of Real Sociedad for nine in the two games; and there followed two creditable wins against Slask Wroclaw — one a 2-1 victory in the depths of a Polish winter. Liverpool went back behind the Iron Curtain for the next round where they faced the East Germans of Dynamo Dresden and a goalless draw in Dresden set them up for a 2-1 home win, although with Dresden scoring that away goal, all minds went back to Ray Clemence's penalty save in East Germany, which proved to be the turning point of the tie.

The semi-final was much tougher but Liverpool came through with flying colours, beating Barcelona 1-0 in Barcelona. The Spaniards boasted the Dutch stars, Cruyff and Neeskens, but Toshack's goal — scored after Keegan knocked on a Clemence goal-kick — was all that Liverpool needed. They followed up with a 1-1 draw at Anfield and went into their second UEFA Cup Final where they met Belgian club Bruges. The first-leg was at Anfield and Liverpool were shocked when Lambert and Cools gave Bruges a 2-0 half-time lead. Although Liverpool fought back to 3-2 through Kennedy,

Steve Heighway – played a key role in Liverpool's march to the 1976 UEFA Cup Final.

Case and a Keegan penalty, it looked like a bad result with only a goal lead to take to Belgium and with two away goals given away into the bargain. Lambert levelled the aggregate after eleven minutes of the second leg but Keegan restored Liverpool's pride with a swerving shot that beat Jensen to win the UEFA Cup.

First Division results 1975-6

Aug 16 QPR .... (a) 0-2
(27,113)
Aug 19 West Ham .... (h) 2-2
(Callaghan, Toshack; 40,564)
Aug 23 Tottenham .... (h) 3-2
(Keegan pen, Case, Heighway; 42,729)
Aug 26 Leeds .... (a) 3-0
(Kennedy, Callaghan 2; 36,186)
Aug 30 Leicester .... (a) 1-1
(Keegan; 25,007)
Sep 6   Sheffield Utd .... (h) 1-0
(Kennedy; 37,340)
Sep 13 Ipswich .... (a) 0-2
(28,132)
Sep 20 Aston Villa .... (h) 3-0
(Toshack, Case, Keegan; 42,779)
Sep 27 Everton .... (a) 0-0
(55,570)
Oct 4   Wolves .... (h) 2-0
(Hall, Case; 36,391)
Oct 11 Birmingham .... (h) 3-1
(Toshack 3; 36,532)
Oct 18 Coventry .... (a) 0-0
(20,695)
Oct 25 Derby .... (h) 1-1
(Toshack; 46,324)
Nov 1   Middlesbrough .... (a) 1-0
(McDermott; 30,952)
Nov 8   Man United .... (h) 3-1
(Heighway, Toshack, Keegan; 49,136)
Nov 15 Newcastle .... (a) 2-1
(Hall, Kennedy; 39,686)
Nov 22 Coventry .... (h) 1-1
(Toshack; 36,929)
Nov 29 Norwich .... (h) 1-3
(Hughes; 34,780)
Dec 2   Arsenal .... (h) 2-2
(Neal 2 pens; 27,447)
Dec 6   Burnley .... (a) 0-0
(18,426)
Dec 13 Tottenham .... (a) 4-0
(Keegan, Case, Neal, Heighway; 29,891)
Dec 20 QPR .... (h) 2-0
(Toshack, Neal pen; 39,182)
Dec 26 Stoke .... (a) 1-1
(Toshack; 32,092)
Dec 27 Man City .... (h) 1-0
(Cormack; 53,386)
Jan 10 Ipswich .... (h) 3-3
(Keegan 2, Case; 40,547)
Jan 17 Sheffield Utd .... (a) 0-0
(31,255)
Jan 31 West Ham .... (a) 4-0
(Toshack 3, Keegan; 26,741)
Feb 7   Leeds .... (h) 2-0
(Keegan, Toshack; 54,525)
Feb 18 Man United .... (a) 0-0
(59,709)
Feb 21 Newcastle .... (h) 2-0
(Keegan, Case; 43,404)
Feb 24 Arsenal .... (a) 0-1
(36,127)
Feb 28 Derby .... (a) 1-1
(Kennedy; 32,800)
Mar 6   Middlesbrough .... (h) 0-2
(41,391)
Mar 13 Birmingham .... (a) 1-0
(Neal pen; 31,397)
Mar 20 Norwich .... (a) 1-0
(Fairclough; 29,013)
Mar 27 Burnley .... (h) 2-0
(Fairclough 2; 36,708)
Apr 3   Everton .... (h) 1-0
(Fairclough; 54,632)
Apr 6   Leicester .... (h) 1-0
(Keegan; 35,290)
Apr 10 Aston Villa .... (a) 0-0
(44,250)
Apr 17 Stoke .... (h) 5-3
(Neal pen, Toshack, Kennedy, Hughes, Fairclough; 44,069)
Apr 19 Man City .... (a) 3-0
(Heighway, Fairclough 2); 50,439)
May 4   Wolves .... (a) 3-1
(Keegan, Toshack, Kennedy; 48,900)

Final League record

P	W	D	L	F	A	Pts	Pos
42	23	14	5	66	31	60	1st

Football League goalscorers: Toshack 16, Keegan 12, Fairclough 7, Case 6, Kennedy 6, Neal 6, Heighway 4, Callaghan 3, Hall 2, Hughes 2, McDermott 1, Cormack 1

FA Cup

Jan 1   (Rnd 3) West Ham .... (a) 2-0
(Keegan, Toshack; 32,363)
Jan 24 (Rnd 4) Derby .... (a) 0-1
(38,200)

FA Cup goalscorers: Keegan, Toshack

Football League Cup

Sep 10 (Rnd 2) York .... (a) 1-0
(Lindsay; 9,421)
Oct 7 (Rnd 3) Burnley........ (h) 1-1
(Case; 24,607)
Oct 14 (replay) Burnley .... (a) 0-1
(19,857)
Football League Cup goalscorers: Lindsay, Case

UEFA Cup

Sep 17 (Rnd 1, 1st leg) Hibs ... (a) 0-1
(12,219)
Sep 30 (Rnd 1, 2nd leg) Hibs .. (h) 3-1
(Toshack 3; 29,963)
Oct 22 (Rnd 2, 1st leg) Real Soc (a) 3-1
(Heighway, Callaghan, Thompson; 30,000)
Nov 4 (Rnd 2, 2nd leg) Real Soc (h) 6-0
(Toshack, Kennedy 2, Fairclough, Heighway, Neal; 23,796)
Nov 26 (Rnd 3, 1st leg) Slask W (a) 2-1
(Kennedy, Toshack; 40,000)
Dec 10 (Rnd 3, 2nd leg) Slask W (h) 3-0
(Case 3; 17,886)
Mar 3 (QF 1st leg)
Dynamo Dresden (a) 0-0
(33,000)
Mar 17 (QF 2nd leg)
Dynamo Dresden (h) 2-1
(Case, Keegan; 39,300)
Mar 30 (SF 1st leg) Barcelona.. (a) 1-0
(Toshack; 80,000)
Apr 14 (SF 2nd leg) Barcelona . (h) 1-1
(Thompson; 55,104)
Apr 28 (Final 1st leg) Bruges .. (h) 3-2
(Kennedy, Case, Keegan pen; 56,000)
May 19 (Final 2nd leg) Bruges.. (a) 1-1
(Keegan; 32,000)
UEFA Cup goalscorers: Toshack 6, Case 5, Kennedy 4, Keegan 3, Thompson 2, Heighway 2, Callaghan 1, Fairclough 1, Neal 1

Kevin Keegan scored in Belgium to ensure that Liverpool would take the UEFA Cup back to Merseyside.

1976-7

There can be no question that 1976-7 is, so far, the greatest season in the great Liverpool story. The Reds retained the First Division championship, won the European Cup, and failed by only a whisker to lift the 'impossible treble' when they lost the 1977 FA Cup Final 2-1 to Manchester United in a thrilling Wembley game. Yet the season could have started on a sorry note for Liverpool fans who learned that their idol, Kevin Keegan, wanted to leave Anfield to try his luck on the Continent. Happily, the Liverpool management and directors persuaded Keegan to stay for one more year, while they tried to lift the European Cup. It was a decision which the player would never regret.

Liverpool's grip on the First Division title was never released. They went to the top on 11 September after beating Derby County 3-2 at the Baseball Ground, were never out of the top three, and eventually took total command of the table on 21 December and remained there until the end of the season, although their record was dimmed somewhat by a 2-1 defeat at Bristol City on the last day of the season, long after the title had been taken again, although the final margin of just one point from Manchester City made it look a closer run affair than it actually was. It was Liverpool's tenth First Division championship and they achieved it with the squad which had won the League and UEFA Cup, plus David Johnson, who arrived at Anfield from Goodison, via Ipswich Town.

Liverpool's European Cup run began with a match against the Irish part-timers of Crusaders who were beaten 2-0 at Anfield and 5-0 in Ulster, although in the Belfast return, Liverpool saw their goalpost hit twice and only four goals in the last nine minutes made the scoreline as one-sided as it eventually was. There were problems in Turkey when Liverpool played Trabzonspor in the second round first-leg tie. Poor facilities saw Liverpool come home trailing 1-0, thanks to a highly-debatable penalty from Trabzonspor midfield player, Cemil. All was put right at Anfield, however, where Liverpool won 3-0 in much more pleasant surroundings. The quarter-final with French champions St Etienne saw Liverpool overturn a first-leg goal deficit and the Anfield crowd saw a thrilling return leg, see-sawing either way before David Fairclough — substituting for Toshack — ran over forty yards to deliver the winner.

David Fairclough scores Liverpool's third goal in the European Cup quarter-final second leg at Anfield on 16 March 1977.

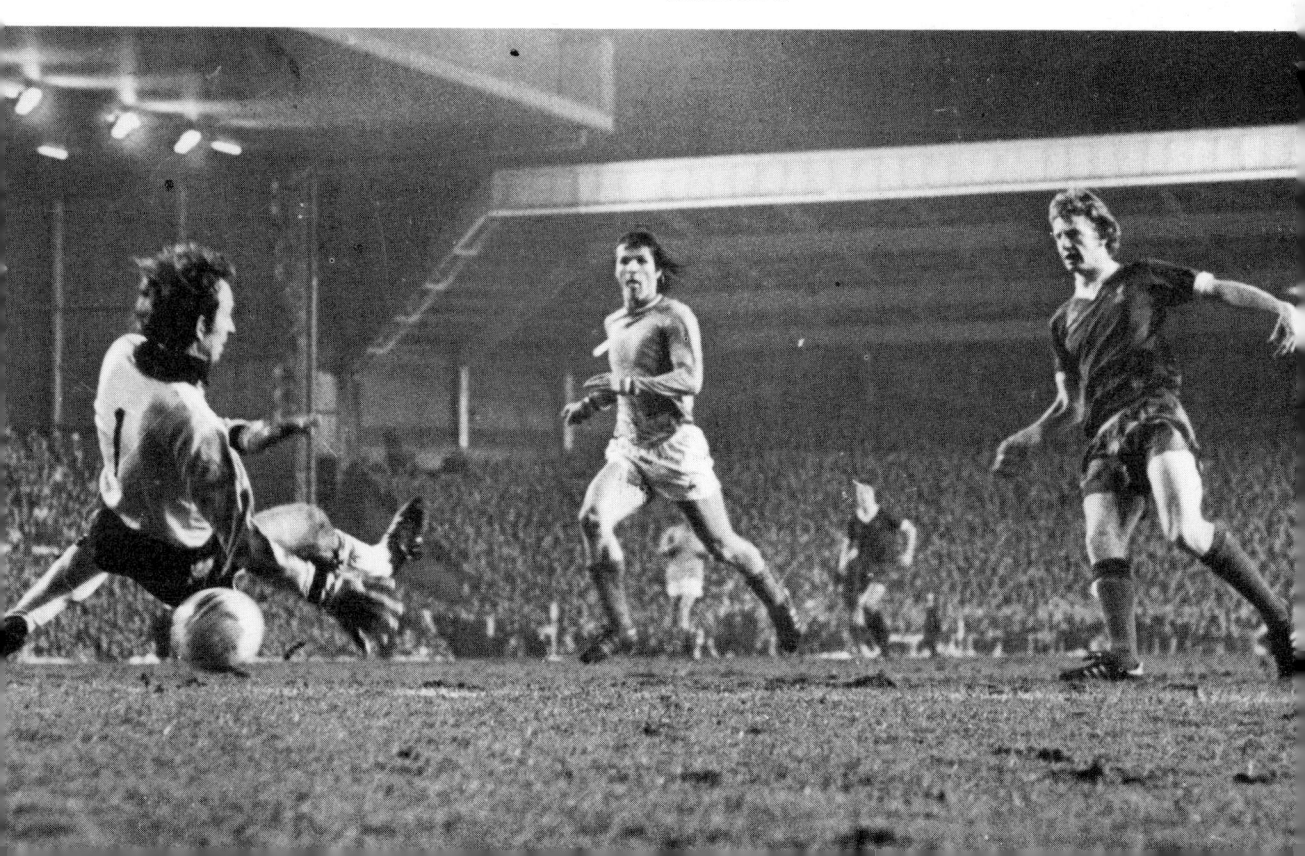

The semi-final against Zurich was a much easier task and Liverpool took little trouble in reaching the European Cup Final — the first English club to do so since Manchester United in 1968.

In Rome, on 25 May 1977, Liverpool brought the European Cup to Anfield by beating Borussia Moenchengladbach 3-1. The Olympic Stadium looked like the Kop itself, with a mass of red and white favours, and after Bonhof had hit the post, Liverpool took the lead through McDermott. Simonsen equalised but then Smith rose high to head home Heighway's corner. Phil Neal coolly stroked home a penalty and Liverpool were champions of Europe. A few days earlier, the Reds had lost the FA Cup to Manchester United, Ray Kennedy hitting the United post with just two minutes to play. Only the woodwork stood between Liverpool and an impossible dream.

First Division results 1976-7

Aug 21 Norwich .... (h) 1-0
(Heighway; 49,753)
Aug 25 West Brom .... (a) 1-0
(Toshack; 30,334)
Aug 28 Birmingham........... (a) 1-2
(Johnson; 33,228)
Sep 4 Coventry .... (h) 3-1
(Keegan, Johnson, Toshack; 40,371)
Sep 11 Derby .... (a) 3-2
(Kennedy, Toshack, Keegan; 26,833)
Sep 18 Tottenham .... (h) 2-0
(Johnson, Heighway; 47,421)
Sep 25 Newcastle .... (a) 0-1
(33,024)
Oct 2 Middlesbrough .... (h) 0-0
(45,107)
Oct 16 Everton .... (h) 3-1
(Heighway, Neal pen, Toshack; 55,141)
Oct 23 Leeds .... (a) 1-1
(Kennedy; 44,696)
Oct 27 Leicester............. (a) 1-0
(Toshack; 29,384)
Oct 30 Aston Villa .... (h) 3-0
(Callaghan, McDermott, Keegan; 51,751)
Nov 6 Sunderland .... (a) 1-0
(Fairclough; 39,956)
Nov 9 Leicester............. (h) 5-1
(Heighway, Toshack, Neal pen, Jones, Keegan pen; 39,851)
Nov 20 Arsenal............... (a) 1-1
(Kennedy; 45,016)
Nov 27 Bristol City .... (h) 2-1
(Keegan, Jones; 44,323)
Dec 4 Ipswich............... (a) 0-1
(35,082)
Dec 11 QPR .... (h) 3-1
(Toshack, Keegan, Kennedy; 37,154)
Dec 15 Aston Villa .... (a) 1-5
(Kennedy; 42,851)
Dec 18 West Ham .... (a) 0-2
(24,175)
Dec 27 Stoke .... (h) 4-0
(Thompson, Neal pen, Keegan, Johnson; 50,371)
Dec 29 Man City .... (a) 1-1
(opp own goal; 50,020)
Jan 1 Sunderland .... (h) 2-0
(Kennedy, Thompson; 44,687)
Jan 15 West Brom .... (h) 1-1
(Fairclough; 39,195)
Jan 22 Norwich .... (a) 1-2
(Neal pen; 25,913)
Feb 5 Birmingham........... (h) 4-1
(Neal pen; Toshack 2, Heighway; 41,072)
Feb 16 Man United .... (a) 0-0
(57,487)
Feb 19 Derby .... (h) 3-1
(Toshack, Jones, Keegan; 44,202)
Mar 5 Newcastle............. (h) 1-0
(Heighway; 45,553)
Mar 9 Tottenham .... (a) 0-0
(32,098)
Mar 12 Middlesbrough .... (a) 1-0
(Hughes; 29,000)
Mar 22 Everton .... (a) 0-0
(56,562)
Apr 2 Leeds .... (h) 3-1
(Neal pen, Fairclough, Heighway; 48,791)
Apr 9 Man City .... (h) 2-1
(Keegan, Heighway; 55,283)
Apr 11 Stoke .... (a) 0-0
(29,905)
Apr 16 Arsenal............... (h) 2-0
(Neal, Keegan; 48,174)
Apr 30 Ipswich............... (h) 2-1
(Kennedy, Keegan; 56,044)
May 3 Man United .... (h) 1-0
(Keegan; 53,046)
May 7 QPR .... (a) 1-1
(Case; 29,832)
May 10 Coventry .... (a) 0-0
(38,032)
May 14 West Ham .... (h) 0-0
(55,675)
May 16 Bristol City .... (a) 1-2
(Johnson; 38,688)

Final League record

P	W	D	L	F	A	Pts	Pos
42	23	11	8	62	33	57	1st

Football League goalscorers: Keegan 12, Toshack 10, Heighway 8, Kennedy 7, Neal 7, Johnson 5, Fairclough 3, Jones 3, Thompson 2, Callaghan 1, Case 1, Hughes 1, McDermott 1, opp own goal 1

FA Cup

Jan 8   (Rnd 3)   Crystal Palace   (h)   0-0
(44,730)
Jan 11   (Replay)   Crystal Palace.   (a)   3-2
(Keegan, Heighway 2; 42,664)
Jan 29   (Rnd 4)   Carlisle ....   (h)   3-0
(Keegan, Toshack, Heighway; 45,358)
Feb 26   (Rnd 5)   Oldham.......   (h)   3-1
(Keegan, Case, Neal pen; 52,455)
Mar 19   (Rnd 6)   Middlesbrough.   (h)   2-0
(Fairclough, Keegan; 55,881)
Apr 23   (SF)   Everton..........   MR   2-2
            (MR = Maine Road)
(McDermott, Case; 52,637)
Apr 27   (Replay)   Everton ......   MR   3-0
(Neal pen, Case, Kennedy; 52,579)
May 21   (Final)   Man United ....   W   1-2
            (W = Wembley)
(Case; 100,000)

FA Cup goalscorers: Keegan 4, Case 4, Heighway 3, Neal 2, Toshack 1, Fairclough 1, Kennedy 1, McDermott 1

Football League Cup

Aug 31   (Rnd 2)   West Brom ....   (h)   1-1
(Callaghan; 23,378)
Sep 6   (replay)   West Brom ....   (a)   0-1
(22,662)

Football League Cup goalscorer: Callaghan

European Cup

Sep 14   (Rnd 1, 1st leg)   Crusaders   (h)   2-0
(Neal pen, Toshack; 22,442)
Sep 28   (Rnd 1, 2nd leg)   Crusaders   (a)   5-0
(Johnson 2, Keegan, McDermott, Heighway; 10,000)
Oct 20   (Rnd 2, 1st leg)
            Trabzonspor ....   (a)   0-1
(25,000)
Nov 3   (Rnd 2, 2nd leg)
            Trabzonspor ....   (h)   3-0
(Heighway, Johnson, Keegan; 42,275)
Mar 2   (QF 1st leg)   St Etienne .   (a)   0-1
(28,000)
Mar 16   (QF 2nd leg)   St Etienne   (h)   3-1
(Keegan, Kennedy, Fairclough; 55,043)
Apr 6   (SF 1st leg)   Zurich.....   (a)   3-1
(Neal 2 (1 pen), Heighway; 30,500)
Apr 20   (SF 2nd leg)   Zurich ....   (h)   3-0
(Case 2, Keegan; 50,611)
May 25   (Final)   Borussia Moen   R   3-1
            (R = Rome)
(McDermott, Smith, Neal pen; 57,000)

European Cup goalscorers: Johnson 4, Neal 4, Keegan 3, Heighway 3, Case 2, McDermott 2, Smith 1, Toshack 1, Kennedy 1, Fairclough 1

Phil Neal's penalty makes it 3-1 to Liverpool in the European Cup Final in Rome on 25 May 1977.

1977-8

How could Liverpool better the achievement of winning the European Cup? The answer was simple, as far as Bob Paisley was concerned — win it again! And that is exactly what the Super Reds did in 1977-8. Liverpool went straight back into Europe and took the magnificent silver trophy down to the European Cup Final at Wembley in May so that they could be re-presented with it and so retain it in the Anfield boardroom for another twelve months.

In the First Division, however, there was a new challenge in the shape of Brian Clough's Nottingham Forest and it was to Trentside that the league championship went, Forest winning it with room to spare. Liverpool made their first-ever appearance in the Football League Cup Final in 1977 — only to be beaten by that team, Nottingham Forest, after a drawn game at Wembley.

Paisley had moved into the transfer market nine days before the season opened, paying Celtic £440,000 for Scottish international striker, Kenny Dalglish, and Dalglish scored his first goal in the opening game of the season at Middlesbrough where Liverpool earned a point in the 1-1 draw. The two First Division meetings with Forest both ended in draws — the game at Anfield being Liverpool's last league match of the season — and Liverpool never topped the First Division during the season, failing (if that is the word) to take the title for the third time in a row.

In the FA Cup they went out 4-2 at Chelsea in only the third round when Clive Walker (2), Tommy Langley and Steve Finnieston scored the goals at Stamford Bridge. It was a surprise result because Chelsea were in the lower half of the table.

Liverpool had never done well in the Football League Cup but they went straight through to the final, pausing only to replay their fourth round match at Coventry. In the semi-final, Ray Kennedy scored the winner against his old club, Arsenal, at Anfield and Liverpool held on 0-0 at Highbury for the right to meet Forest. The first match at Wembley was a goalless draw after Dalglish missed a fairly easy chance to end the deadlock, and the teams retired to Old Trafford for the replay. Controversy surrounded the winning goal of that game, scored by John Robertson from the penalty spot after Phil Thompson was ruled to have brought down a Forest forward. There was less debate about the foul, than about where it was committed. Replayed television film suggested that Thompson had felled O'Hare *outside* the penalty area, before the Forest player tumbled into the eighteen-yard box. Nevertheless, it was a penalty and Forest took the League Cup back to the City Ground.

Horror on Liverpool faces as Borussia Moenchengladbach snatch a last-minute goal in the first leg of the European Cup semi-final in West Germany in March 1978.

But in Europe, Liverpool marched on and on. Dynamo Dresden, Benfica and Borussia Moenchengladbach were each removed from the competition. The final was at Wembley but Bruges, former UEFA Cup Final opponents of Liverpool, never wanted to make a game of it and it took a delicate chip from Kenny Dalglish to separate the teams at the end of the day. Liverpool were European champions for the second successive season, which meant a crack at the hat-trick next season, despite the fact that they had lost the league to Forest. It would soon be Forest's turn to wrest the European championship from Anfield.

First Division results 1977-8

Aug 20 Middlesbrough (a) 1-1 (Dalglish; 31,000)
Aug 23 Newcastle (h) 2-0 (Dalglish, McDermott; 48,267)
Aug 27 West Brom (h) 3-0 (Dalglish, Heighway, Case; 48,525)
Sep 3 Birmingham (a) 1-0 (Kennedy; 28,239)
Sep 10 Coventry (h) 2-0 (Fairclough, Dalglish; 45,574)
Sep 17 Ipswich (a) 1-1 (Dalglish; 29,658)
Sep 24 Derby (h) 1-0 (McDermott; 48,359)
Oct 1 Man United (a) 0-2 (55,109)
Oct 4 Arsenal (a) 0-0 (47,110)
Oct 8 Chelsea (h) 2-0 (Dalglish, Fairclough; 40,499)
Oct 15 Leeds (a) 2-1 (Case 2; 45,500)
Oct 22 Everton (h) 0-0 (51,668)
Oct 29 Man City (a) 1-3 (Fairclough; 49,207)
Nov 5 Aston Villa (h) 1-2 (opp own goal; 50,436)
Nov 12 QPR (a) 0-2 (25,625)
Nov 19 Bristol City (h) 1-1 (Dalglish; 41,053)
Nov 26 Leicester (a) 4-0 (Fairclough, Heighway, Dalglish, McDermott; 26,051)
Dec 3 West Ham (h) 2-0 (Dalglish, Fairclough; 39,659)
Dec 10 Norwich (a) 1-2 (Thompson; 24,983)
Dec 17 QPR (h) 1-0 (Neal pen; 38,249)
Dec 26 Nottm Forest (a) 1-1 (Heighway; 47,218)
Dec 27 Wolves (h) 1-0 (Neal pen; 50,294)
Dec 31 Newcastle (a) 2-0 (Thompson, Dalglish; 35,302)
Jan 2 Middlesbrough (h) 2-0 (Johnson, Heighway; 49,305)
Jan 14 West Brom (a) 1-0 (Johnson; 35,809)
Jan 21 Birmingham (h) 2-3 (Thompson, Kennedy; 48,401)
Feb 4 Coventry (a) 0-1 (28,965)
Feb 25 Man United (h) 3-1 (Souness, Kennedy, Case; 49,590)
Mar 4 Chelsea (a) 1-3 (Neal pen; 33,550)
Mar 8 Derby (a) 2-4 (Fairclough, Dalglish; 23,413)
Mar 11 Leeds (h) 1-0 (Dalglish; 48,233)
Mar 25 Wolves (a) 3-1 (Case, Dalglish 2; 27,531)
Apr 1 Aston Villa (a) 3-0 (Dalglish 2, Kennedy; 40,190)
Apr 5 Everton (a) 1-0 (Johnson; 52,759)
Apr 8 Leicester (h) 3-2 (Smith 2, Lee; 42,979)
Apr 15 Bristol City (a) 1-1 (Heighway; 31,471)
Apr 18 Ipswich (h) 2-2 (Dalglish, Souness; 40,044)
Apr 22 Norwich (h) 3-0 (Fairclough 2, opp own goal; 44,857)
Apr 25 Arsenal (h) 1-0 (Fairclough; 38,318)
Apr 29 West Ham (a) 2-0 (McDermott, Fairclough; 37,448)
May 1 Man City (h) 4-0 (Dalglish 3, Neal pen; 44,528)
May 4 Nottm Forest (h) 0-0 (50,021)

Final League record

P	W	D	L	F	A	Pts	Pos
42	24	9	9	65	34	57	2nd

Football League goalscorers: Dalglish 20, Fairclough 10, Heighway 5, Case 5, Kennedy 4, Neal 4, McDermott 4, Thompson 3, Johnson 3, Souness 2, Smith 2, Lee 1, own goals 2

FA Cup

Jan 7 (Rnd 3) Chelsea .... (a) 2-4
(Johnson, Dalglish; 45,449)

FA Cup goalscorers: Johnson, Dalglish

Football League Cup

Aug 30 (Rnd 2) Chelsea .... (h) 2-0
(Dalglish, Case; 33,170)
Oct 26 (Rnd 3) Derby .... (a) 2-0
(Fairclough 2; 30,400)
Nov 29 (Rnd 4) Coventry ...... (h) 2-2
(Fairclough, Neal pen; 33,817)
Dec 20 (replay) Coventry ...... (a) 2-0
(Case, Dalglish; 36,105)
Jan 17 (Rnd 5) Wrexham ..... (a) 3-1
(Dalglish 3; 25,641)
Feb 7 (SF 1st leg) Arsenal.... (h) 2-1
(Dalglish, Kennedy; 44,764)
Feb 14 (SF 2nd leg) Arsenal ... (a) 0-0
(49,561)
Mar 18 (Final) Nottm Forest... (W) 0-0
(W = Wembley)
(100,000)
Mar 22 (replay) Nottm Forest .. (MC) 0-1
(MC = Man United)
(54,375)

Football League Cup goalscorers: Dalglish 6, Fairclough 3, Case 2, Neal 1, Kennedy 1

European Cup

Oct 19 (Rnd 2, 1st leg)
  Dynamo Dresden ... (h) 5-1
(Hansen, Case 2, Neal pen, Kennedy; 39,835)
Nov 2 (Rnd 2, 2nd leg)
  Dynamo Dresden ... (a) 1-2
(Heighway; 33,000)
Mar 1 (QF 1st leg) Benfica ... (a) 2-1
(Case, Hughes; 70,000)
Mar 15 (QF 2nd leg) Benfica... (h) 4-1
(Callaghan, Dalglish, McDermott, Neal; 48,364)
Mar 29 (SF 1st leg)
  Borussia Moen ..... (a) 1-3
(Johnson; 67,000)
Apr 12 (SF 2nd leg)
  Borussia Moen ..... (h) 3-0
(Kennedy, Dalglish, Case; 51,500)
May 10 (Final) Bruges......... (W) 1-0
  (W = Wembley)
(Dalglish; 92,000)

European Cup goalscorers: Case 4, Dalglish 3, Neal 2, Kennedy 2, Hansen 1, Heighway 1, Hughes 1, Callaghan 1, McDermott 1, Johnson 1

We did it again! Emlyn Hughes holds aloft the European Cup for the second successive season.

European Cup Final at Wembley, 10 May 1978. A Graeme Souness shot shaves the Bruges post.

1978-9

It was Nottingham Forest — the team which was to prove Liverpool's 'bogey' side — who stood in the Reds' path as they tried to take the European Cup again. The sides met as early as the first round and Forest won their home first-leg with a goal from the hitherto unknown Garry Birtles, and one from Colin Barrett. Liverpool never got to grips with Forest in the return leg and the goalless draw meant that Liverpool were out — although the trophy remained in England when Forest went on to win it in Munich.

Sheffield United's Gary Hamson scored the goal which defeated Liverpool in the second round of the Football League Cup at Bramall Lane, and it was the First Division championship and the FA Cup which Liverpool were left with as the season was less than two months old.

The Reds responded magnificently. By the time the third round of the FA Cup came round in January, Liverpool were miles ahead at the top of the table where they had been since the third game of the season. Even snow, ice and waterlogged pitches — which extended the season — failed to upset their momentum. They lost only four matches — to Arsenal, Aston Villa, Bristol City and Everton — and conceded only sixteen goals — the best-ever peformance by a Football League defence in one season. They also scored a massive eighty-five goals and the title was theirs by eight points from Forest. Liverpool had now won the First Division championship eleven times — three more than the next club, Arsenal. The average attendance at Anfield had been 46,406 and away from home the record-breaking Reds had pulled in almost 776,000 — an average away gate of nearly 37,000. It was a magnificent performance which underlined the sheer professional dedication, character and skill of the entire Anfield machine.

Emlyn Hughes and Paul Mariner (Ipswich) chase the ball during the match between Liverpool and the Suffolk club on 22 August 1978.

In the FA Cup Liverpool went nearly all the way, losing their replayed semi-final 1-0 to Manchester United. Liverpool found themselves at Southend in the third round where the seaside team managed a fine goalless draw before losing 3-0 at Anfield; Kenny Dalglish disposed of Blackburn Rovers in an all-Lancashire fourth round, and two goals from David Johnson and one from Graham Souness beat another local challenger in the shape of Burnley. Dalglish it was who put paid to Ipswich Town's hopes and Liverpool were semi-finalists once more.

At Maine Road, Manchester, Liverpool and Manchester United made a 2-2 draw, Dalglish and Hansen scoring for Liverpool and Joe Jordan and Brian Greenhoff hitting the United goals. Although Hansen's equaliser had come late in the game, McDermott missed a penalty and twice Liverpool gave United another chance when they failed with easy chances. Liverpool supporters looked forward to the replay at Everton with obvious relish. But their faith was misplaced. Liverpool's defence was far shakier than the 1-0 scoreline suggests and Jimmy Greenhoff's late goal only gave United the result that they deserved — not the scoreline. But Liverpool were champions again and into the European Cup for another year, so making the Super Reds England's most experienced European campaigners.

First Division results 1978-9

Aug 19 QPR .... (h) 2-1
(Dalglish, Heighway; 50,793)

Aug 22 Ipswich .... (a) 3-0
(Souness, Dalglish 2; 28,114)

Aug 26 Man City .... (a) 4-1
(Souness 2, R. Kennedy, Dalglish; 46,710)

Sep 2 Tottenham .... (h) 7-0
(Dalglish 2, R. Kennedy, Johnson 2, Neal pen, McDermott; 50,705)

Sep 9 Birmingham .... (a) 3-0
(Souness 2, A. Kennedy; 31,740)

Sep 16 Coventry .... (h) 1-0
(Souness; 51,130)

Sep 23 West Brom .... (a) 1-1
(Dalglish; 38,000)

Sep 30 Bolton .... (h) 3-0
(Case 3; 47,099)

Oct 7 Norwich .... (a) 4-1
(Heighway 2, Johnson, Case; 25,632)

Oct 14 Derby .... (h) 5-0
(Johnson, R. Kennedy 2, Dalglish 2; 47,475)

Oct 21 Chelsea .... (h) 2-0
(Johnson, Dalglish; 45,775)

Bob Paisley and Kenny Dalglish celebrate another First Division title after the match with Aston Villa on 8 May 1979.

Oct 28 Everton .... (a) 0-1
(53,131)
Nov 4 Leeds .... (h) 1-1
(McDermott pen; 51,657)
Nov 11 QPR .... (a) 3-1
(Heighway, R. Kennedy, Johnson; 26,626)
Nov 18 Man City .... (h) 1-0
(Neal pen; 47,765)
Nov 22 Tottenham .... (a) 0-0
(50,393)
Nov 25 Middlesbrough .... (h) 2-0
(McDermott, Souness; 39,821)
Dec 2 Arsenal .... (a) 0-1
(51, 902)
Dec 9 Nottm Forest .... (h) 2-0
(McDermott 2 (1 pen); 51,469)
Dec 16 Bristol City .... (a) 0-1
(28,722)
Dec 26 Man United .... (a) 3-0
(R. Kennedy, Case, Fairclough; 54,940)
Feb 3 West Brom .... (h) 2-1
(Dalglish, Fairclough; 52,211)
Feb 13 Birmingham .... (h) 1-0
(Souness; 35,207)
Feb 21 Norwich .... (h) 6-0
(Dalglish 2, Johnson 2, A. Kennedy, R. Kennedy; 35,754)
Feb 24 Derby .... (a) 2-0
(Dalglish, R. Kennedy; 27,859)
Mar 3 Chelsea .... (a) 0-0
(40,594)
Mar 6 Coventry .... (a) 0-0
(26,629)
Mar 13 Everton .... (h) 1-1
(Dalglish; 52,352)
Mar 20 Wolves .... (h) 2-0
(McDermott, Johnson; 39,695)
Mar 24 Ipswich .... (h) 2-0
(Dalglish, Johnson; 43,243)
Apr 7 Arsenal .... (h) 3-0
(Case, Dalglish, McDermott; 47,297)
Apr 10 Wolves .... (a) 1-0
(Hansen; 30,857)
Apr 14 Man United .... (h) 2-0
(Dalglish, Neal; 46,608)
Apr 16 Aston Villa .... (a) 1-3
(Johnson; 44,029)
Apr 21 Bristol City .... (h) 1-0
(Dalglish; 43,191)
Apr 24 Southampton .... (a) 1-1
(Johnson; 23,181)

Apr 28 Nottm Forest .... (a) 0-0
(41,898)
May 1 Bolton .... (a) 4-1
(Johnson, R. Kennedy 2, Dalglish; 35,200)
May 5 Southampton .... (h) 2-0
(Neal 2; 46,687)
May 8 Aston Villa .... (h) 3-0
(A. Kennedy, Dalglish, McDermott; 50,570)
May 11 Middlesbrough .... (a) 1-0
(Johnson; 32,244)
May 17 Leeds .... (a) 3-0
(Johnson 2, Case; 41,324)

Final League record

P	W	D	L	F	A	Pts	Pos
42	30	8	4	85	16	68	1st

Football League goalscorers: Dalglish 21, Johnson 16, R. Kennedy 10, Souness 8, McDermott 8, Case 7, Neal 5, Heighway 4, A. Kennedy 3, Fairclough 2, Hansen 1

FA Cup

Jan 10 (Rnd 3) Southend ..... (a) 0-0
(31,033)
Jan 17 (replay) Southend ..... (h) 3-0
(Case, Dalglish, R. Kennedy; 37,797)
Jan 30 (Rnd 4) Blackburn ..... (h) 1-0
(Dalglish; 43,432)
Feb 28 (Rnd 5) Burnley .... (h) 3-0
(Johnson 2, Souness; 47,161)
Mar 10 (Rnd 6) Ipswich .... (a) 1-0
(Dalglish; 31,322)
Mar 31 (SF) Man United ...... MC 2-2
         (MC = Man City)
(Dalglish, Hansen; 52,584)
Apr 4 (Replay) Man United .. E 0-1
(53,069) (E = Everton)

FA Cup goalscorers: Dalglish 4, Johnson 2, Case 1, R. Kennedy 1, Souness 1, Hansen 1

Football League Cup

Aug 28 (Rnd 2) Sheffield Utd .. (a) 0-1
(35,753)

European Cup

Sep 13 (Rnd 1, 1st leg)
(38,316)   Nottm Forest ...... (a) 0-2
Sep 27 (Rnd 1, 2nd leg)
(51,679)   Nottm Forest ...... (h) 0-0

1979-80

Liverpool just keep marching on! Despite the disappointment of their European Cup dismissal, and the eventual slips in both the FA Cup and the Football League Cup, the Super Reds went on to take the First Division title for the twelfth time and so extend their record of championship wins. For much of the season Liverpool's right to another title seemed without doubt. And even after the hiccups of the run-in to the season, when Manchester United looked as though they might spring a shock, the fact remained that Liverpool were rightful champions, although the final margin of just two points was much slimmer than the gap which the Anfield club had opened up earlier in the season.

In the two domestic cup competitions, Liverpool reached both semi-finals. The League Cup run started as near to home as possible with a draw at Tranmere Rovers in the first leg of the second round before Liverpool steamrollered their less-illustrious Merseyside neighbours at Anfield. Chesterfield and Exeter gave Liverpool little trouble, Norwich were removed efficiently at Carrow Road, and then the Reds faced their old bogey team in Brian Clough's Nottingham Forest. The sides were due to meet three times in close succession because Liverpool had also been drawn away at the City Ground in the FA Cup. In the League Cup Forest took the honours, winning 1-0 in Nottingham and then holding Liverpool 1-1 at Anfield to take Clough's side into their third consecutive League Cup Final at Wembley.

But in between that two-legged League Cup semi-final defeat Liverpool did manage to lay the Forest bogey when Dalglish and McDermott (from the penalty spot) gave them a 2-0 FA Cup fourth round win at the City Ground. It was the start of a long cup run. David Fairclough netted both the goals as Lancashire neighbours Bury were beaten 2-0 in the fifth round; and McDermott scored the only goal of the sixth round tie with Tottenham Hotspur at White Hart Lane. Then came the semi-final with Arsenal — a semi-final which left Football Association administrators sweating at the prospect of the tie not being decided until it was too late to make arrangments for the May 10 Wembley final. Alas, for Liverpool, it was decided in Arsenal's favour and instead of an all-Merseyside final, we had an all-London affair.

The thought of Irish champions Dundalk going further in the European Cup than mighty Liverpool is something to make the average soccer fan scoff in disbelief. But that is exactly what happened in

Terry McDermott celebrates his first goal in the 1979 Charity Shield game against Arsenal at Wembley.

1979-80 as Liverpool went tumbling out in the first round to Russian champions Dynamo Tbilisi. Liverpool missed the midfield expertise of the injured Ray Kennedy for the first leg and only rank bad finishing by the Russians prevented them from taking a sensational victory. As it was, Liverpool could only take a 2-1 lead to Russia and there the Dynamo team hammered the Reds 3-0 and they were out 4-2 on aggregate.

But Liverpool will be competing in the European Cup next season and there can surely be nothing to stop this red tide from sweeping into the Continent with renewed fervour. Liverpool keep coming near to that fantastic feat of lifting every trophy in sight. Perhaps the 'eighties will be their decade for final and absolute domination.

Kenny Dalglish.

First Division Results 1979-80

Aug 21 Bolton (h) 0-0 (45,900)
Aug 25 West Brom (h) 3-1 (Johnson 2, McDermott; 48,021)
Sep 1 Southampton (a) 2-3 (Johnson, Irwin; 21,402)
Sep 8 Coventry (h) 4-0 (Johnson 2, Case, Dalglish; 39,926)
Sep 15 Leeds (a) 1-1 (McDermott; 39,779)
Sep 22 Norwich (h) 0-0 (44,120)
Sep 29 Nottm Forest (a) 0-1 (28,262)
Oct 6 Bristol City (h) 4-0 (Johnson, Dalglish, R. Kennedy, McDermott; 38,213)
Oct 9 Bolton (a) 1-1 (Dalglish; 25,571)
Oct 13 Ipswich (a) 2-1 (opp own goal, Johnson; 25,310)
Oct 20 Everton (h) 2-2 (opp own goal, R. Kennedy; 52,201)
Oct 27 Man City (a) 4-0 (Johnson, Dalglish 2, R. Kennedy; 48,128)
Nov 3 Wolves (h) 3-0 (Dalglish 2, R. Kennedy; 49,541)
Nov 10 Brighton (a) 4-1 (R. Kennedy, Dalglish 2, Johnson; 29,692)
Nov 17 Tottenham (h) 2-1 (McDermott 2; 51,092)
Nov 24 Arsenal (a) 0-0 (55,561)
Dec 1 Middlesbrough (h) 4-0 (McDermott, Hansen, Johnson, R. Kennedy; 39,885)
Dec 8 Aston Villa (a) 3-1 (R. Kennedy, Hansen, McDermott; 41,160)
Dec 15 Crystal Palace (h) 3-0 (Case, Dalglish, McDermott; 42,898)
Dec 22 Derby (a) 3-1 (opp own goal, McDermott, Johnson; 24,945)
Dec 26 Man United (h) 2-0 (Hansen, Johnson; 51,073)
Dec 29 West Brom (a) 2-0 (Johnson 2; 34,915)
Jan 12 Southampton (h) 1-1 (McDermott; 44,655)
Jan 19 Coventry (a) 0-1 (31,578)
Feb 9 Norwich (a) 5-3 (Fairclough 3, Dalglish, Case; 25,624)
Feb 19 Nottm Forest (h) 2-0 (McDermott, R. Kennedy; 45,093)
Feb 23 Ipswich (h) 1-1 (Fairclough; 47,566)

Feb 26 Wolves .... (a) 0-1
(36,693)
Mar 1   Everton .... (a) 2-1
(Johnson, Neal; 53,013)
Mar 11 Man City .... (h) 2-0
(opp own goal, Souness; 40,443)
Mar 15 Bristol City .... (a) 3-1
(R. Kennedy, Dalglish 2; 27,187)
Mar 19 Leeds .... (h) 3-0
(Johnson 2, A. Kennedy; 37,008)
Mar 22 Brighton............. (h) 1-0
(Hansen; 42,747)
Mar 29 Tottenham .... (a) 0-2
(32,114)
Apr 1   Stoke .... (h) 1-0
(Dalglish; 36,415)
Apr 5   Man United .... (a) 1-2
(Dalglish; 57,342)
Apr 8   Derby .... (h) 3-0
(Irwin, Johnson, opp own goal; 40,932)
Apr 19 Arsenal.............. (h) 1-1
(Dalglish; 46,878)
Apr 23 Stoke .... (a) 2-0
(Johnson, Fairclough; 32,000)
Apr 26 Crystal Palace .... (a) 0-0
(45,583)
May 3   Aston Villa .... (h) 4-1
(Johnson 2, Cohen, opp own goal; 51,541)
May 6   Middlesbrough .... (a) 0-1
(24,458)

Phil Thompson takes good care of the 1980 First Division Championship trophy.

Final League record

P	W	D	L	F	A	Pts	Pos
42	25	10	7	81	29	60	1st

League goalscorers: Johnson 21, Dalglish 16, McDermott 11, R. Kennedy 9, Fairclough 5, Hansen 4, Case 3, Irwin 2, Neal 1, Souness 1, A. Kennedy 1, Cohen 1, opp own goals 6

FA Cup

Jan 5   (Rnd 3) Grimsby ...... (h) 5-0
(Souness, Johnson 3, Case; 49,706)
Jan 26 (Rnd 4) Nottm Forest .. (a) 2-0
(Dalglish, McDermott; 33,277)
Feb 16 (Rnd 5) Bury .... (h) 2-0
(Fairclough 2; 43,769)
Mar 8   (Rnd 6) Tottenham .... (a) 1-0
(McDermott; 48,033)
Apr 12 (SF) Arsenal .... (n) 0-0
(50,174)
Apr 16 (replay) Arsenal .... (n) 1-1
(Fairclough; 40,679)
Apr 28 (replay) Arsenal .... (n) 1-1
(Dalglish; 42,975)
May 1   (replay) Arsenal .... (n) 0-1
(35,335)

FA Cup goalscorers: Johnson 3, Fairclough 3, Dalglish 2, McDermott 2, Souness 1, Case 1

League Cup

Aug 29 (Rnd 2, 1st leg) Tranmere (a) 0-0
(16,759)
Sep 4   (Rnd 2, 2nd leg) Tranmere (h) 4-0
(Thompson, Dalglish 2, Fairclough; 24,785)
Sep 25 (Rnd 3) Chesterfield ... (h) 3-1
(Fairclough, Dalglish, McDermott; 20,960)
Oct 30 (Rnd 4) Exeter .... (h) 2-0
(Fairclough 2; 21,019)
Dec 5   (Rnd 5) Norwich ...... (a) 3-1
(Johnson 2, Dalglish; 23,000)
Jan 22 (SF 1st leg) Nottm Forest (a) 0-1
(32,234)
Feb 12 (SF 2nd leg) Nottm Forest (h) 1-1
(Fairclough; 50,880)

League Cup scorers: Fairclough 5, Dalglish 4, Johnson 2, McDermott 1, Thompson 1

European Cup

Sep 19 (Rnd 1, 1st leg)
        Dynamo Tbilisi..... (h) 2-1
(Johnson, Case; 35,270)
Oct 3   (Rnd 1, 2nd leg)
        Dynamo Tbilisi..... (a) 0-3
(80,000)

European Cup goalscorers: Johnson, Case

TWELVE GREAT REDS

BILL SHANKLY's life and his contribution to English football in general and Liverpool in particular, would take at least two volumes to record. He was born in Ayrshire and played with Carlisle United and Preston North End as a fierce wing-half, winning five Scottish caps. He played in the FA Cup Finals of 1937 and 1938, winning a cup-winners medal in his second appearance. He guided Liverpool to just about every honour in the game and his dry sense of humour, incredible commitment to the game, and great managerial skills have made him one of soccer's most beloved characters. Suffice to say, 'There is only *one* Bill Shankly'.

BILLY LIDDELL's honours in the game do not measure up to his incredible ability and reputation. His fifteen seasons produced only a League-Championship medal in 1946-7 and an FA Cup runners-up medal in 1949-50. Yet, if he was around today, Liddell would fetch at least one million pounds on the transfer market. His first season for Liverpool (he was recommended by Matt Busby) produced seven goals in thirty-four games as the Reds won the title. By the time he retired in 1960, Liddell had scored 216 goals for Liverpool in 492 games, and in addition, won twenty-eight Scotland caps, together with two appearances for the Great Britain side. He was never sent off and was booked only once in his career — although he once gave England goalkeeper Frank Swift such a powerful shoulder-charge that Swift broke two ribs! Liddell served Liverpool well both on the football pitch and in civic life when he became a JP.

ROGER HUNT was one of the most prolific goalscorers ever to play for Liverpool. He signed for them in 1959-60 and in that first season scored twenty-one goals in thirty-six matches. A native of the Warrington area, Hunt went on to win a World Cup winners medal with England in 1966 as well as League Championship medals with Liverpool in 1963-4 and 1965-6, and an FA Cup winners medal in 1965. When Hunt won a Second Division championship medal in 1961-2, he also broke the Liverpool individual scoring record with forty-one goals in the season. Hunt's exceptional ability to be in the right place at the right time made him an automatic choice for Liverpool and when he left them for Bolton Wanderers in 1969-70, he had played over 400 games for the Reds and scored 245 goals. He also won thirty-four England caps, scoring eighteen goals for his country. His testimonial game between the Liverpool 1965 Cup winning side and an England XI was watched by over 56,000 fans who turned out to pay homage to this great footballer.

IAN CALLAGHAN was born in Liverpool and made his debut for the Reds as a seventeen-year-old winger in April 1960. He played in four league games that season and only three the season after that. But from that moment, Ian Callaghan became a fixture in the Liverpool side until, at the end of the 1977-8 season, he had clocked up 636 Football League matches for the club, plus four as substitute, and had scored forty-nine goals during that time. He made his England debut against Finland in 1966 and played four times in the full international side, making further appearances against France, Switzerland, and Luxembourg. Callaghan started his career as a winger — on his debut in the 4-0 win over Bristol Rovers the other players applauded him off the pitch — but his greatest days at Anfield were perhaps as a midfield player. Altogether, he broke Billy Liddell's record of 513 first team appearances for the Anfield club.

PETER THOMPSON was born in Carlisle and played with Preston North End before joining Liverpool. A brilliant schoolboy footballer who had already pulled on the white shirt of his country, Thompson also made his league debut at the age of seventeen when Preston played him against Arsenal in August 1960. Preston were destined to be relegated that season but Deepdale fans were already talking of the 'new Tom Finney'. The Second Division, however, did not suit him and he played in every forward position before Liverpool rescued him on 14 August 1963 — just three years after he had made his debut. In that first season with Liverpool, Thompson won four under-23 England caps and six full caps, making his international debut against Portugal in Lisbon on 17 May and playing throughout England's summer tour. Thompson played over 300 league games for Liverpool and scored over forty goals. He was always a fast and dangerous winger. Just as Preston fans had seen him as their new Tom Finney, so Liverpool supporters felt they had a new Billy Liddell.

TONY HATELEY spent only one full season with Liverpool but that is not surprising when one considers that he seemed to be perpetually on the move during the 'sixties. Yet in that one season, 1967-8, Hateley scored sixteen goals in thirty-nine matches as well as creating havoc in quite a few First Division defences as he helped Liverpool to finish in third place. Hateley was born in Derby and first played for Notts County. There followed spells with Aston Villa and Chelsea and, after Liverpool, Coventry, Birmingham and Notts County again. A big, agile striker, Hateley was ideal for 'aerial warfare' and even though he played only four games in 1968-9 before going to Highfield Road, he still managed to score a goal. Hateley now lives on Merseyside and his son Mark is making a name for himself with Coventry City, managed by another ex-Liverpool stalwart, Gordon Milne.

RAY CLEMENCE's career started in the unglamourous surroundings of Third Division Scunthorpe United's Old Show Ground when he made four appearances for them in 1965-6. A native of Skegness, Clemence left the wastelands of the Third Division the following season for the First Division trappings of Liverpool. After two years in the Reds Central League side, Clemence made his First Division debut in 1969-70 and played fourteen times for the first team. The following season he went through the campaign as Liverpool's first-choice goalkeeper and has now made over 400 League appearances to become the country's leading goalkeeper. He made his England debut in 1973 against Wales and has now won over fifty England caps, despite the fact that Peter Shilton has often pushed him hard for a place. Clemence is a natural goalkeeper — and a modest one; his only reply to the comment that he is the best was, 'There are no bad goalkeepers in the First Division'.

STEVE HEIGHWAY got his big chance when Bill Shankly's Liverpool was ravaged by injuries during the first half of the 1970-1 season. The moustached, Dublin-born winger with a university degree, took that chance with both feet and since then has played some 400 games for Liverpool, scoring over sixty goals. Heighway's first season saw him play thirty-three times in Liverpool's league programme and in 1971 he made his debut for the Republic of Ireland against Poland and since then has played for his country nearly thirty times. A Bachelor of Arts from Warwick University, Heighway is known to his Liverpool teammates as 'Big Bamber' after television egg-head, Bamber Gascoigne (Liverpool's Brian Hall, a BSc from Liverpool University, was 'Little Bamber').

TOMMY SMITH's approach to the game of football says much about the Liverpool attitude which has made the club such a great force in European football. Smith made his debut in 1962-3, playing just one match, and it was 1964-5 before he became a regular member of the Liverpool first team. A powerful wing-half, Smith strode the fields of Europe, always in the forefront of the Liverpool battle, although he was capped only once by England when he appeared against Wales in 1971. Playing alongside Ron Yeats, Smith shored up the middle of the Liverpool defence, a role he was to continue to play throughout his career. Tommy Smith was the concrete of the Liverpool wall. He made well over 500 appearances in the red shirt of his home club.

KEVIN KEEGAN's match appearance statistics may appear insignificant in comparison with many other players who have pulled on the famous red jersey of the Anfield club hundreds more times, but for Kop fans all over the world, Kevin Keegan *was* Liverpool. Signed from Scunthorpe United in 1971, Keegan's contribution to the great Liverpool sides of the mid-Seventies cannot be measured by statistics alone and it was a sad day for the club when he chose to try his fortune in West Germany. He made his England debut against Wales in 1973 and has gone on to captain his country, ensuring that even after his transfer to S. V. Hamburg, he would still be able to play in international matches. He has made over fifty England appearances and when he left Liverpool at the end of 1976-7 season, Keegan had played 230 league games and scored sixty-eight goals. He has now returned to England to play for Southampton.

RAY KENNEDY was already an established First Division star when Liverpool signed him from Arsenal in 1974 for £200,000 but it was at Anfield that the midfield player won a place in the England side. Kennedy was Bill Shankly's last signing before the old lion retired from the fray. Kennedy has played over 200 league games for Liverpool alone and scored over forty goals during those appearances. He was born at Seaton Delavel and before moving to Anfield had made 156 league appearances for the Highbury club, plus two as a substitute. He is rated one of England's best midfielders.

EMLYN HUGHES is yet another great name in the story of Liverpool Football Club. Hughes had made a handful of appearances for Blackpool (he was actually born at Barrow-in-Furness) when Bill Shankly signed him as a nineteen-year-old defender in time for 1967-8. Hughes went on to captain Liverpool to League, FA Cup and European triumphs and he played fifty-nine times for England while at Anfield, making his international debut against Wales in 1970. When he signed for Wolverhampton Wanderers in 1979, Hughes had played in more than 500 Liverpool games.